Renate Luscher

Deutsch ganz leicht **A1**

Selbstlernkurs Deutsch für Anfänger

A German Self-Study Course for Beginners

Zweisprachiges Arbeitsbuch

Bilingual Workbook

Englische Bearbeitung

John Stevens

Hueber Verlag

Quellenverzeichnis

Umschlagcover: Paar © iStockphoto/undergroundw, Gendarmenmarkt © panthermedia/Corinna H.

Seite 37:   MHV-Archiv (Heribert Mühldorfer)

Seite 75:   links außen: © PhotoDisc; Mitte links und rechts außen: MHV-Archiv
(Dieter Reichler); Mitte rechts: MHV-Archiv (Gerd Pfeiffer)

4. 3. 2. | Die letzten Ziffern
2018 17 16 15 14 | bezeichnen Zahl und Jahr des Druckes.
Alle Drucke dieser Auflage können, da unverändert,
nebeneinander benutzt werden.
1. Auflage
© 2011 Hueber Verlag GmbH & Co. KG, Ismaning, Deutschland
Redaktion: Marion Kerner, Hans Hillreiner, Hueber Verlag, Ismaning
Umschlaggestaltung: creative partners gmbh, München
Satz, Layout und Grafik: Martin Lange, Karlsfeld
Zeichnungen: Marlene Pohle, Stuttgart
Druck und Bindung: Kessler Druck + Medien GmbH & Co. KG, Bobingen
Printed in Germany
ISBN 978–3–19–507480–3 (Paket)
52.7480 (Buch)

Contents

How to work with *Deutsch ganz leicht*

Dear Learner of German,

You have acquired a German self-study course and are setting out to learn a language that is the mother tongue of 100 million people. To help you make rapid and solid progress, I'll give you a brief introduction to the course. In the package you'll find:

1. a Bilingual Workbook,
2. a Textbook and
3. two Audio-CDs.

The *Workbook* is your manual that will guide you step by step through the course. It is important that you always read the instructions in the Workbook first before you continue. Here's Lesson 1 as a model:

p. 5/6 + p. 5-7

Dialogue with exercises:
Work with the Textbook (= T) and the Workbook (= A) side by side. In the Workbook you'll find the pictograms of the listening texts and the translations of the instructions.

p. 7-8

Grammar – New Words – Exercises:
Continue working in the Workbook following the numbering. The Workbook contains thorough explanations of the grammar which is just sketched out on notepad sheets in the Textbook.

p. 9

Pronunciation:
Also in the Workbook you'll find exercises on pronunciation features.

p. 8 + p. 9

Cultural Info:
To round off the lesson you'll do a game-like activity, for instance solving a puzzle. This is always on the last page of the lesson in the Textbook. You'll find translations and explanations in the Workbook.

p. 10

Test:
The Test at the end of each lesson will tell you whether you should go back and revise something or can continue.

The appendix contains the complete answer key and glossary. If you don't understand or have forgotten a word, look it up in the glossary. That's the quickest way to learn it. By the end of the course you'll know 900 words, and have learned enough to be able to communicate well in everyday situations, make phone calls and write simple letters.

So have fun now and enjoy yourself. And another final tip: don't listen to people who claim German is a difficult language to learn. We'll soon show you that the opposite is true!

With best wishes,
Renate Luscher

Guten Tag oder Hallo! – Hello and Hi

Four people – Jürgen Heinrich, Chris Bruckner, Rob Klein and Claudia Bergmann – are going to accompany you through this language course. At the beginning of Lesson 1 we're in Berlin, at the airport and at the station. Chris Bruckner has just arrived from Munich for a business meeting. Robert wants to have a look round Berlin. He's being met at the station by Claudia.

In Lesson 1 you'll learn how to greet somebody and say goodbye to them, and what the difference between *du* and *Sie* is, and also how you introduce somebody else.

1 *Please match.*

Please do exercise 1 in the textbook as preparation for the first dialogue: Guten Tag *is the standard form of greeting at any time of the day. Among friends people often just say* Hallo.

Guten Morgen!	*Good morning!*
Guten Abend!	*Good evening!*
(Gute Nacht!)	*(Good night)!*
Auf Wiedersehen!	*Goodbye!*
Tschüs!	*Bye!*

2 This is Jürgen Heinrich, Chris Bruckner, Robert and Claudia

1A

→ *Listen to how the four of them greet each other. Frau Bruckner and Herr Heinrich haven't met before, but Robert and Claudia already know each other of course. Listen to the conversation at least twice.*

→ *Read the dialogue in the textbook.*

→ *Listen to the text and read the dialogue at the same time.*

→ *Now underline the stressed syllables.*

Guten Tag. Sind Sie Herr Heinrich?
Ja, das bin ich.
Mein Name ist Bruckner, Chris Bruckner.
Guten Tag, Frau Bruckner. Herzlich willkommen.

→ *Read the dialogue out loud following your underlinings.*

→ *Then turn to the vocabulary section. Try to learn the meaning of the words and the sentences by heart.*

Guten Tag,	*Hello/Good morning/afternoon,*
sind Sie Herr Heinrich?	*are you Mr Heinrich?*
Ja, das bin ich.	*Yes, I am.*
ja	*yes*
ich bin	*I am*
Mein Name ist Bruckner.	*My name is Bruckner.*

Frau Bruckner	Mrs Bruckner
Guten Tag, Frau Bruckner.	Hello, Frau Bruckner.
Herzlich willkommen.	Welcome.

1B

→ Listen to part 1B.
→ Read the dialogue in the textbook.
→ Listen to the text and read the dialogue at the same time.
→ Now underline the stressed syllables.

Hallo, Rob.
etc.

→ Read the dialogue out loud following your underlinings.
→ Then turn to the vocabulary section.

Hallo, Rob/Claudia.	Hi Rob/Claudia.
Wie geht's dir/Ihnen?	How are you? (informal/formal)
Danke, gut.	Fine, thanks.

3 Listen. What is the order?

4 What goes together?
There is one answer for each sentence. Link the question and answer.

5 Please complete.
Complete the greetings when people say Sie or du to each other.

Sie or du?
When you address someone else you use Sie or du.
People use du when talking to relatives or friends, or when students are talking among themselves. Sometimes people who work together use it, too, but only in work-places where this is the normal thing to do. Sie is the polite and non-intrusive form of address and is the correct one to use in all other cases.

6 Please complete.
Fill in the forms of sein. They are very important. The forms are unfortunately all irregular.

7 What fits? Listen and mark.

8 What fits? Please write.

Now we're going to practise some grammar (grammar = Grammatik; exercises = Übungen).
As you do so, you'll also be extending your vocabulary (new words = Neue Wörter).

sein (be): Sie sind – du bist (both: you are)

Singular	1. Person	ich	**bin**	
	2. Person	du	**bist**	aus München, Berlin,
	3. Person	er/sie	**ist**	Köln, Stuttgart ...
Plural	1. Person	wir	**sind**	
	2. Person	ihr	**seid**	
	3. Person	sie/Sie	**sind**	

	Sie/Sie	du/ihr
Singular	Sind Sie aus ...?	Bist du aus ...?
	(= Herr Heinrich)	(= Robert)
Plural	Sind Sie aus ...?	Seid ihr aus ...?
	(= Herr und Frau Heinrich)	(= Robert und Claudia)

9 *Please match.*

| Das bin | Das ist | Das sind | Das seid |

Sie   wir   ihr   sie (Sing.)

ich   er   sie (Pl.)

10 *Complete the sentences by writing in the missing forms.*

Ich _____ aus Barcelona.

_____ Sie aus Rom?

_____ du aus Warschau?

Herr Heinrich _____ aus Berlin.

Wir _____ aus Moskau.

_____ ihr aus London?

_____ Sie aus Rio?

11 *Wie geht's dir?*
There are three drawings. The people are talking. How do you think they greet each other?
Choose the correct answer.

Grüß Gott.

| Grüß Gott. | Danke, Frau Müller. | Tag auch. | Wie geht's? |

Hallo, Claudia, hallo, Evelyn, wie geht's?

| Grüß Gott, Nina. | Gut, und dir? | Aha. |

Grüezi.

| Grüezi, Nina. | Servus. | Gut, und dir? |

 Listen to the dialogues and check your answers.

12 *Revision*
Note these expressions. It would be best to learn them by heart.

Greeting someone / introducing yourself

Formal

Guten Tag, Frau/Herr + Nachname	*Good morning/afternoon/evening,* *Frau/Herr + surname*
Mein Name ist … (Bruckner/Heinrich).	*My name is … (Bruckner/Heinrich).*
Ich bin … (Chris Bruckner/Jürgen Heinrich).	*I am … (Chris Bruckner/Jürgen Heinrich).*
Ich heiße … (Bruckner/Heinrich).	*My name is … (Bruckner/Heinrich).*
Wie geht es Ihnen?	*How are you?*
Danke, gut. (Und Ihnen?)	*Fine, thanks. (And you?)*

 Here's a tip: The expression *Mein Name ist …* is very formal. Only use it with your surname: *Mein Name ist Bruckner.* The more common and informal expression is *Ich heiße …*, e.g. *Ich heiße Chris Bruckner.* And by the way: people don't usually say: *Ich heiße Frau Bruckner.*

Informal

Hallo + Vorname	*Hello + first name*
Ich bin … / Ich heiße …	*I'm … / My name's …*
Wie geht's? Wie geht's dir?	*How are you?*
Danke, gut. (Und dir?)	*Fine, thanks. (And you?)*

Introducing someone

Das ist Herr Berger.	*This is Herr Berger.*
Guten Tag, Herr Berger. Ich bin Klaus Nagel.	*Hello, Herr Berger. I'm Klaus Nagel.*

13 *Listen and repeat what you hear.*
You already know the words and phrases. Try and imitate the speaker's stress and pronunciation as closely as you can.

Bruckner	Frau Bruckner	Guten Tag, Frau Bruckner.
Heinrich	Herr Heinrich	Guten Tag, Herr Heinrich.
Mein Name	Mein Name ist …	Mein Name ist Bruckner.
Ich	Ich heiße …	Ich heiße Heinrich.
Willkommen	Herzlich willkommen	Herzlich willkommen, Frau Bruckner.
Wie	Wie geht's?	Wie geht's Ihnen?
Danke	gut	Danke, gut.

14 *The Alphabet*
Now we're going to practise sounds. Listen and repeat. Try and copy the speaker's pronunciation as closely as possible.

Aa	eF	Ka	Oo	eS	We
Be	Ge	eL	Pe	Te	iX
Ce	Ha	eM	Qu	Uu	Ypsilon
De	Ii	eN	eR	Vau	Zet
Ee	Jot				

15 *Special Sounds*
German has some special sounds – the umlauts ä, ö, ü, and ß (= eszet). Repeat the following words and imitate the speaker as closely as possible.

Ö ö	schön *(nice)*
Ü ü	Glück *(luck)*
Ä ä	Geschäft *(business)*
ß	ich heiße

Try and spell your name. You won't have any trouble with that, will you?

Cultural info (Textbook page 8)

Here's a summary of how people greet each other and say goodbye in Northern and Southern Germany, Austria and Switzerland. Of course there are many more regional forms. But these can be heard very often.

Auf Wiedersehen.	*Goodbye.*
Tschüs.	*Bye/Cheers/See you.*
Adieu.	*Goodbye/Bye.*
Ciao.	*See you.*

Listen and compare.

Vocabulary

1. Mark the right translation with a cross.

1. Guten Tag.
☑ Hello.
☐ Good afternoon.
☐ Good morning.

2. Guten Morgen.
☐ Hello.
☐ Good afternoon.
☑ Good morning.

3. Hallo.
☑ Hello.
☐ Good morning.
☐ Hi.

4. Wie geht's Ihnen?
☐ Where are you from?
☑ How are you?
☐ Who are you?

5. Danke, gut.
☑ Fine, thanks.
☐ And you, too.
☐ See you.

6. Auf Wiedersehen.
☐ Welcome.
☑ Goodbye.
☐ Hello.

2. Please complete.

1. Guten _Tag_ !
2. Auf _Wiedersehen_ !
3. _Guten_ Tag!

4. _Guten_ Abend!
5. _Guten_ Morgen!
6. Tsch _uß_ !

Grammar

3. Fill in the forms of sein.

1. ich _____
2. du _____
3. er _____
4. sie (= Claudia) _____

5. Das _____ Robert.
6. _____ Sie Herr Bermann?
7. _____ Sie Frau Bergmann?
8. _____ Sie Herr und Frau Bergmann?

4. Please complete.

1. Ich _____ Julia.
2. _____ du Erik?
3. _____ Sie Herr Schmidt?

4. Ich _____ Wolfgang Schmidt.
5. Mein Name _____ Berger.
6. Das _____ Herr Berger.

Check your answers in the key at the back of the book and then add up your points.

Total:		
	1 – 13	Before you carry on, you really should do this lesson again.
	14 – 22	Quite good, but not perfect yet. Please go over the dialogues and the grammar again.
	23 – 26	Very good. You can carry straight on.

Woher kommen Sie? – Where do you come from?

Herr Heinrich takes Frau Bruckner to his office via the hotel. From their conversation on the way you find out more about them.

When you want to get to know somebody, you have to ask questions. So in Lesson 2 you are going to learn how to ask questions. That's relatively easy in German.

1 *To prepare for the conversation, have a look at the map (Textbook, page 8). Find the cities Berlin, München (Munich), Wien (Vienna), etc. and say out loud* Da ist … . *Three of the cities are mentioned in the dialogue.*

2 Herr Heinrich and Frau Bruckner in the car

→ *Listen to Herr Heinrich's and Frau Bruckner's conversation.*

→ *Listen to the conversation at least twice.*

→ *Read the dialogue in the textbook.*

→ *Listen to the text and read the dialogue at the same time.*

→ *Now underline the stressed syllables.*

1|10

Sind Sie aus Berlin, Herr Heinrich?
etc.

→ *Then read the dialogue out loud following your underlinings.*

→ *Then turn to the vocabulary section. Try to learn the meaning of the words and the sentences by heart.*

Sind Sie …?	*Are you …?*
aus Berlin	*from Berlin*
Kommen Sie …?	*Do you come …?*
Wohnen Sie …?	*Do you live …?*
Leben Sie …?	*Do you live …?*
Ja, klar.	*Yes, of course.*
Und Sie,	*And you,*
woher kommen Sie?	*where do you come from?*
Aus Österreich,	*From Austria,*
ich bin aus Wien.	*I am from Vienna.*
aber	*but*
ich lebe	*I live*
ich komme	*I come*
ich kenne	*I know*
in München	*in Munich*
schon lange	*a long time*
Sind Sie gern in …?	*Do you like it in …?*
sehr gern	*(like) a lot*
ich wohne	*I live*

schon fünf Jahre	*for five years*
dort	*there*
Kennen Sie …?	*Do you know …?*
Ja, aber nicht gut.	*Yes, but not well.*

3 *Mark the verb.*

4 *What fits?*
Now listen to the text again und check your answers.

5 *Questions put to Chris Bruckner. Mark the right answer.*

6 *Please answer. What is correct?*

7 *We ask – you answer*
Imagine somebody asks you personally how you are. Listen, then select your answer and say it out loud.

If you say *Na ja*, people know immediately that you don't feel too good.
If you start with *Ach*, it's a sign that you're going to say you don't feel good at all.

8 *Write the verbs.*
The Sie form is always the same as the infinitive.

Please write. What is the question/answer?

lebt	Pierre	Paris	in	_____ ?

in	Paris	ja	er	lebt	_____ .

aus	Paris	er	ist	_____ .

kennen	Paris	Sie	_____ ?

nicht	ja	gut	aber	_____ .

kenne	London	ich	gut	_____ .

These grammar explanations include information on the differences between German and English usage, whenever relevant.

Verbs in the present – Verben im Präsens

Singular	1. Person	ich	komme	aus München, Berlin, Köln, Stuttgart ...
	2. Person	du	kommst	
	3. Person	er / sie	kommt	
Plural	1. Person	wir	kommen	
	2. Person	ihr	kommt	
	3. Person	sie / Sie	kommen	

- Unlike in English, the ending of the verb changes with the person (*ich, du, er* etc.), though some persons share the same ending (*wir kommen, sie kommen*).
- Other verbs that have the same ending as *kommen* are: *kennen, leben, wohnen, heißen* (Note: *du heißt*).
- The infinitive has the ending *-(e)n*. This is the form you find in a dictionary. It is also the form you know from the instructions: *Hören Sie. Schreiben Sie* etc.

9 *Underline the infinitives.*

| bist | heiße | sein | kenne | seid | lebe | wohnen |

| lebt | kennst | komme | heißen | wohnt | kennen |

10 *Complete the table by writing in the missing forms.*

		kennen	**leben**	**wohnen**	**heißen**
Singular	ich	kenne	lebe	wohne	
	du		lebst		heißt
	er / sie	kennt	lebt		heißt
Plural	wir	kennen	leben		heißen
	ihr		lebt	wohnt	heißt
	sie / Sie	kennen		wohnen	

11 *Fill in the forms of* heißen.

Ich heiße _____ _____ (= Ihr Name).

Wie _____ du?   Wir _____ Knut und Boris.

Er _____ Boris.   Wie _____ ihr?

Wie _____ Sie? Neumann?   Karla und Fritz _____ Sauter.

13

Questions with and without question words – Fragen mit und ohne Fragewort

There are questions with and without question words. *Woher* is a question word.

Woher **kommen Sie**?	–	**Aus** Berlin / England / Italien.
Woher **kommst du**?	–	**Aus** München / Polen / Frankreich.
Kommen Sie aus Italien?	–	Ja, ich komme **aus** Italien.
Kommst du aus Polen?	–	Nein, ich komme **aus** Frankreich.

Questions are easy to form in German. You just turn the subject (= the person doing the action) and the verb round. So *Sie kommen* becomes *Kommen Sie* in a question.

12 *Here are lots of questions and answers. Write the correct form of the verb in the gap.*

Woher _____ (kommen) Andrea?

Aus Berlin. Sie _____ (kommen) aus Berlin.

_____ (leben) Pierre in München?

Nein, in Paris. Pierre _____ (leben) in Paris.

Woher _____ (kommen) Graziella
und Paolo? Aus Verona?

Ja, sie _____ (kommen) aus Verona.

_____ (wohnen) Juan auch in Verona?

Nein, Juan _____ (wohnen) in Madrid.

_____ (kennen) Sie Warschau?

Ja, ich _____ (kennen) Warschau gut.

_____ (wohnen) Elsbeta in Warschau?

Ja, sie _____ (wohnen) in Warschau.

13 *Revision*
Note these expressions. It would be best to learn them by heart.

Asking where someone comes from

Woher sind / kommen Sie? Woher bist / kommst du?	*Where are you from? / Where do you come from?*
Ich bin / komme aus … (Berlin / München / Österreich).	*I am / come from … (Berlin / Munich / Austria).*
Aus … (Berlin / München / Österreich).	*From … (Berlin / Munich / Austria).*
Sind Sie aus … (München / Österreich)? Bist du aus … (München / Österreich)?	*Are you from … (Munich / Austria)?*
Ja, ich bin aus …	*Yes, I'm from …*
Nein, ich bin aus …	*No, I am from …*
Leben / Wohnen Sie in … (Berlin / München)?	*Do you live in … (Berlin / Munich)?*
Ja, ich lebe / wohne in …	*Yes, I live in …*
Nein, ich lebe / wohne in …	*No, I live in …*
Ich bin schon fünf Jahre in …	*I have been in … for five years.*
Kennen Sie … (Berlin / München)?	*Do you know … (Berlin / Munich)?*
Ja, aber nicht gut.	*Yes, but not well.*

14 *Listen and repeat.*
You already know the words and phrases. Try and imitate the speaker's stress and pronunciation as closely as you can.

Aus Berlin. — Sind Sie aus Berlin?
Aus Wien. — Ich bin aus Wien.
In München. — Aber ich lebe in München.
schon fünf Jahre — Ich wohne schon fünf Jahre dort.
kennen — Kennen Sie Berlin?
nicht gut — Ja, aber nicht gut.

15 *Repeat the names of the cities and countries.*

Zürich	Leipzig	Salzburg
Frankfurt	Hamburg	Augsburg
Berlin	Wien	Paris
Köln	Bern	Graz
Deutschland	Österreich	die Schweiz

16 a. *Listen.*
Three young people – Nina, Achim and Christian – are greeting each other.

Nina: Hallo, ich bin Nina, und du?
Achim: Ich heiße Achim. Hallo!
Nina: Kommst du auch aus Berlin?
Achim: Nein, aus München, ich bin schon lange in München.
Christian: Ich bin Christian.
Achim: Tag, Christian.
Christian: Tag.
Achim: Woher bist du?
Christian: Aus Hamburg.
Achim: Aha.

16 b. *Now listen to the dialogue a second time and read the sentences at the same time. Try and imitate the speaker's stress as closely as you can.*

Cultural info: City quiz (Textbook page 12)

In addition to the capital cities Berlin and Vienna, here are some other important cities. You can look and see on the map where they are.
Auerbach's Cellar: One of the ten most famous restaurants in the world. Made famous by Goethe's Faust.

What's the name of the city?
Write the names of the cities.

Vocabulary

1. Mark the right translation.

1.
Wie geht's?
☐ How are you?
☐ Where are you from?
☐ How do you do?

2. (Kommen Sie aus Berlin?)
– Ja, klar.
☐ Yes, I am from Berlin.
☐ Yes, of course.
☐ Really?

3. (Sind Sie Herr / Frau ...?)
– Ja, das bin ich.
☐ I'm ...
☐ Yes, I am.
☐ Yes, please.

2. Give the correct translation.

1. to come _____

2. to live _____

3. to be called _____

4. to be _____

5. to know _____

| kennen |
| kommen |
| leben / wohnen |
| heißen |
| sein |

Grammar

3. Underline the correct form.

1. Kommst du auch [in] [aus] [im] Berlin?
2. [Kommst] [Kommen] [Kommt] Sie aus England?
3. Ich [wohne] [leben] [komme] schon lange in München.
4. Und woher kommen [Sie] [er] [ich] ?
5. [Kennst] [Kennen] [Kenne] Sie Hamburg?
6. [Kommt] [Kommen] [Kommt] Sie auch aus Norddeutschland?

4. What's the question?

1. [Sie] [kommen] [woher]   _____ ?
2. [Sie] [aus Hamburg] [sind]   _____ ?
3. [in München] [wohnen] [Sie] _____ ?
4. [Berlin] [Sie] [kennen]   _____ ?
5. [Sie] [sind] [Herr Müller]   _____ ?
6. [geht es] [wie] [Ihnen]   _____ ?

Check your answers in the key at the back of the book and then add up your points.

Total:
1 – 10	It would be a good idea to do this lesson again straightaway.
11 – 17	Pretty good. But it wouldn't hurt to go over the dialogues and the grammar again.
18 – 20	Excellent. If you like, you could go over the vocabulary again, otherwise you can carry straight on.

Im Hotel – At the Hotel

Frau Bruckner checks in at her hotel. She has to fill in the registration form and supply her personal details.

In this lesson you're going to learn a lot about nouns. A special feature of German is the fact that all nouns are written with a capital letter. There is also a capital letter at the beginning of a sentence, and proper names are also written with a capital: *Mein Name ist Müller.*

1 *Please match.*
Please do exercise 1 as preparation for the lesson. Here is a summary of nouns that are important when giving personal details. Match the terms.
If you want to make things a bit easier, you can start with the following translation exercise. Please match the terms and their translations.
Note: postcodes in Berlin start with a 1...

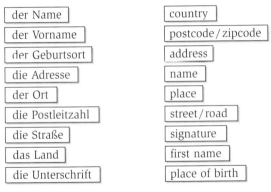

der Name	country
der Vorname	postcode / zipcode
der Geburtsort	address
die Adresse	name
der Ort	place
die Postleitzahl	street / road
die Straße	signature
das Land	first name
die Unterschrift	place of birth

Do you notice anything? Yes, of course. There are words in German and English that have the same root: *the name – der Name, the address – die Adresse* and many more.

2 Checking in at the hotel
This is Frau Bruckner's business card. First listen to the words and then fill in the hotel registration form.

3 *What's your name? Fill in the registration form for yourself.*
You are now the hotel guest.

4 *Ask and answer: What fits?*
Maybe the receptionist has asked for your personal details. Match the questions to the details on the form.

5 *What belongs together? Write the noun with its article.*
All nouns have an article. In German there are three different articles: der, die, das.

Always learn nouns together with their article, so learn *der Name*, not just *Name*. Store article and noun in your memory as a unit that belongs together. That will help you avoid a lot of mistakes.

6 *What's the word?*
This requires a good memory. So let's relax a bit with a little puzzle.

7 *A form – Please fill in.*

Familienname	*family name, surname*
Vorname / Vornamen	*first name / first names*
Geburtsname	*maiden name, name at birth*
Geburtsland	*country of birth*
Geburtsdatum	*date of birth*
Tag	*day*
Monat	*month*
Jahr	*year*
Familienstand	*marital status*
ledig	*single*
verheiratet	*married*
geschieden	*divorced*
Geschlecht	*sex*
männlich	*male*
weiblich	*female*
Nationalität	*nationality*
Platz	*place*
Nummer	*number*
Stadt	*town*
Pass-Nummer	*passport number*
Ausweis-Nummer	*identity card number*
Datum	*date*

8 *What belongs together?*
Draw lines.

9 *Write your name, where you come from and where you live.*
Try and say the sentence out loud. You're bound to be asked sometime.

10 aus *and* in
aus *and* in *are used in combination with certain verbs. Fill in the appropriate preposition.*

There are certain points to note about the names of countries if you want to avoid mistakes.

Ländernamen – Names of countries

without an article	with an article		
	der	die	Plural
China	der Libanon	die Schweiz	die Niederlande
Japan	der Sudan	die Türkei	die USA
Österreich	(der) Irak		
Polen	(der) Iran		
Spanien	(der) Jemen		
Deutschland usw.			

Most names of countries don't have an article. It's easiest if you just note the exceptions.

11 *Please complete.*
A lot of names of countries end in -ien. Is your country one of them? Write the name in English next to each country.

Arg _ _ _ _ _ ien   _____   Ind _ _ esien _____

Austr _ _ ien   _____   Ita _ ien   _____

Bel _ _ en   _____   Kro _ _ _ en _____

Bra _ _ _ ien   _____   Molda _ ien _____

Bul _ _ rien   _____   Rum _ nien _____

Groß _ _ _ _ _ nien _____   Sl _ _ enien _____

I _ dien   _____

Woher kommen Sie / kommst du?	– **Aus** Österreich / Deutschland / Spanien / Russland / Japan / Australien. Aber: **Aus der** Schweiz/**Aus den** USA. **Aus (dem)** Irak / **Aus (dem)** Iran / **Aus dem** Sudan.
Wo wohnen Sie / wohnst du?	– **In** Österreich/Deutschland/Spanien/ Russland / Japan / Australien. Aber: **In der** Schweiz/**In den** USA. **Im/In** Irak / **Im/In** Iran / **Im** Sudan.

12 *Complete the name of the country.*
You can see from the name where the person comes from.

Woher kommt ...

... Tatjana?   Aus R _ _ _ land.   ... Paul?   Aus _ _ _ _ _ _ _ _ _ _ _.

... Michel?   Aus F _ _ _ _ reich.   ... Urs?   Aus der _ _ _ _ _ _ _ _.

... Susan?   Aus den _ _ _ .   ... Eri Enaba? Aus J _ _ _ _ _ .

Numbers – Zahlen

0 null	3 drei	6 sechs	9 neun
1 eins	4 vier	7 sieben	10 zehn
2 zwei	5 fünf	8 acht	

13 *Start at 0 and draw a line to the next number until you get to 10. Then write the numbers down in the right order.*

___null___ _____ _____ _____ _____ _____ _____

_____ _____ _____ _____ _____

14 *Write down the postcodes. Then listen and compare.*

sieben null eins neun null   _ _ _ _ _   Stuttgart

acht null acht null fünf   _ _ _ _ _   München

sieben sechs eins drei sieben   _ _ _ _ _   Karlsruhe

sechs null drei eins drei   _ _ _ _ _   Frankfurt am Main

sechs neun eins eins acht   _ _ _ _ _   Heidelberg

zwei null eins vier drei   _ _ _ _ _   Hamburg

15 *Revision*
Here are some important questions and requests:

Entschuldigung, ich habe eine Frage.	*Excuse me, I have a question.*
Was bedeutet das?	*What does this mean?*
Was bedeutet das Wort?	*What does the word mean?*
Was bedeutet der Satz?	*What does the sentence mean?*
Wie heißt das auf Deutsch?	*What is that in German?*
Bitte buchstabieren Sie.	*Please spell it.*
Bitte langsam.	*Slowly please.*
Bitte sprechen Sie langsam.	*Please speak slowly.*
Bitte sprechen Sie nicht so schnell.	*Please don't speak so fast.*
Bitte wiederholen Sie.	*Please repeat.*

In German these phrases don't sound as abrupt as in English.

16 *Listen and repeat what you hear.*
You already know the words and phrases. Try and imitate the speaker's stress and pronuncia-
tion as closely as you can.

Woher	Woher kommst du?
Wo	Wo bist du geboren?
Wo	Wo wohnst du?
Wie	Wie heißt du?
Wie	Wie geht's dir?
Was	Was ist das?

17 *Listen and repeat.*
Numbers 0 – 10: You'll find the numbers on page 20.

18 *For bright sparks.*
If you're good in working things out, you'll have no problems with this. Read the four
numbers in each line, then fill in the last number.

eins	zwei	drei	vier	_____
zehn	acht	sechs	vier	_____
acht	sieben	sechs	fünf	_____
eins	drei	fünf	sieben	_____

19 *Postcodes. Repeat the question.*

Wo ist 20103?	Das ist in Hamburg.
Wo ist 69317?	Das ist in Frankfurt.
Wo ist 69118?	Das ist in Heidelberg.
Wo ist 10117?	Das ist in Berlin.
Wo ist 80637?	Das ist in München.

Cultural info (Textbook page 16)

People who look as though they're foreigners often aren't. Often they were born in
Germany and have a German passport.

What does the reporter say? What does the man say?
Write the dialogue.

Now listen and compare.

Vocabulary

1. *Mark the right translation.*

1. Wie ist Ihr Name?
☐ How are you?
☐ What's your name?
☐ Tell me your name.

2. Wo sind Sie geboren?
☐ When were you born?
☐ Where were you born?
☐ What's your place and date of birth?

3. Bitte buchstabieren Sie.
☐ Please repeat.
☐ Please spell it.
☐ Please don't speak so fast.

4. Ich bin geschieden.
☐ I'm married.
☐ I'm divorced.
☐ I'm single.

5. Woher …?
☐ Where … from?
☐ Who …?
☐ Where …to?

6. Die Pass-Nummer bitte.
☐ Your passport number, please.
☐ The date of issue of your passport, please.
☐ The password, please.

2. *Supply the article.*

1. _____ Land   3. _____ Adresse   5. _____ Pass

2. _____ Stadt   4. _____ Ort   6. _____ Visum

Grammar

3. *Please complete.*

1. Sind Sie _____?

2. Wo _____ _____?

3. Wie ist _____ _____?

4. Woher _____ _____?

5. Ist das _____ _____?

6. Kommen Sie _____ _____?

| wohnen Sie |
| kommen Sie |
| aus Österreich |
| Ihre Adresse |
| verheiratet |
| die Pass-Nummer |

Listening Comprehension

(1|25)

4. *Listen to the short dialogue and mark the right answers.*

1. Der Mann heißt
☐ Müller.
☐ Janssen.

2. Die Frau heißt
☐ Janssen.
☐ Müller.

3. Die Frau kommt aus
☐ Berlin.
☐ Hamburg.

Check your answers in the key at the back of the book and then add up your points.

Total:	1 – 11	Oh dear, it's a pity. Please do this unit again.
	12 – 18	Not so bad. But even so, it would be a good idea to go over the vocabulary and the grammar again.
	19 – 21	Excellent. There's nothing to stop you carrying on.

Smalltalk

We are now in Herr Kühne's office. Chris Bruckner has an appointment with him.
You'll hear some small talk about a journey and the weather, and will learn how to ask
"how are you?" and to reply to this.

1 *Please do exercise 1 in the textbook as preparation for the dialogue. Are you missing some vocabulary items? Here are the translations.*

Wie geht's?	How are you?
Wie ist das Wetter?	What's the weather like?
Wie ist das Hotel?	What's the hotel like?
Wie war die Reise?	How was the trip?
Gut, danke. / Es geht.	Fine, thanks. / Not too bad.
Nicht sehr gut. Leider.	Not very good, I'm afraid.
Das ist prima.	That's great.

2 Frau Bruckner and Herr Kühne in the office   1|26

4A

→ *Now listen to Herr Kühne greeting Frau Bruckner. They talk about her journey and the weather of course. Listen to the conversation at least twice.*

→ *Read the dialogue in the textbook.*

→ *Listen to the text and read the dialogue at the same time.*

→ *Underline the stressed syllables.*

Guten Tag, Frau Bruckner. Wie geht's?   Auch gut. Und nicht weit.
Wie war die Reise?   Sie sind ja direkt im Zentrum.
Guten Tag, Herr Kühne. Danke, gut.   Ja, das ist sehr praktisch.
Und wie ist das Hotel?

→ *Read the dialogue out loud following your underlinings.*

→ *Then turn to the vocabulary section. Try to learn the meaning of the words and the sentences by heart.*

Reise (die)	trip, journey
weit	far
Sie sind ja direkt im Zentrum.	You're right in the centre.
Zentrum (das)	centre
praktisch	handy, practical

The question: *Wie war die Reise?* is a frequent expression and a good one for starting a conversation.

4B

→ *Listen to part 4B.*
→ *Read the dialogue in the textbook.*
→ *Listen to the text and read the dialogue at the same time.*
→ *Now underline the stressed syllables.*
→ *Read the dialogue out loud following the stressed syllables.*
→ *Then turn to the vocabulary section.*

Das Wetter ist auch prima.	*The weather's great, too.*
Wetter (das)	*weather*
prima – schön – warm	*fine, great – fine, beautiful – warm*
Wie ist es denn in München?	*What's it like in Munich?*
Leider schlecht.	*Bad, I'm afraid.*
schlecht	*bad*
Es regnet schon zwei Tage.	*It's been raining for two days.*
regnen – es regnet	*rain*
Da haben Sie hier Glück.	*You're lucky here.*
Glück (das)	*luck*
Dann machen wir eine Stadtrundfahrt.	*Then we'll do a city tour.*
machen – er / sie macht	*do, make*
Stadtrundfahrt (die)	*city tour*
Vielleicht morgen?	*Maybe/ Perhaps tomorrow?*
Ja, gerne.	*Gladly./ I'd like that.*

3 *Listen to the dialogue. Mark the person.*

4 *What's right? What's wrong? Mark accordingly.*

5 *Read the dialogue.*

6 *What's right?*

7 *An interview – First read the answers. Then listen and answer accordingly.*
As preparation please do the following exercise, then exercise 7 in the textbook will be no problem. Please complete.

Positiv					Negativ
sehr gut	gut	nicht so gut	nicht (sehr) gut	schlecht	sehr schlecht
sehr schön	_____	_____	_____	schlecht	_____

8 *Listen, and write the adjectives.*

Now we're going to do a bit of grammar practice. We're going to concentrate on nouns and articles that are very typical of German.

Article + Noun – Artikel + Nomen

Every noun has its article.

People	Article + Noun		Personal Pronoun
Jürgen Heinrich	**der** Name	→	er
Chris Bruckner	**die** Adresse	→	sie
	das Land	→	es

In German all nouns are written with a capital letter. That makes it easy to spot them. Unlike English, German has three different articles. Unfortunately there's no hard and fast rule that says which article goes with which noun.

9 *Note down all the nouns from Dialogue 4.*

_____   _____   _____   _____

_____   _____   _____   _____

_____   _____   _____

10 *Fill in the article.*

_____ Reise   _____ Land   _____ Stadt   _____ Stadtrundfahrt

_____ Zentrum   _____ Name   _____ Hotel   _____ Glück

_____ Adresse   _____ Tag   _____ Wetter

11 *Fill in the right personal pronoun. The article will help you.*
For example: das Wetter → es

das Geschäft – _____	der Euro – _____	das Auto – _____
der Tag – _____	die Reise – _____	die Zeit – _____
die Stadt – _____	das Haus – _____	die Adresse – _____

yes/no questions – Negation with *nicht*		**Ja/Nein-Fragen – Die Verneinung mit *nicht***
Ist das Frau Bruckner?	–	**Ja**, das ist Frau Bruckner.
Ist das Herr Heinrich?	–	**Nein**, das ist **nicht** Herr Heinrich.
Wie ist das Wetter in München?	–	Es ist sehr **schön**.
Wie ist das Wetter in Berlin?	–	Es ist **nicht schön**.
Kennen Sie Berlin gut?	–	**Ja**, ich kenne Berlin **gut**.
Kennen Sie München gut?	–	**Nein**, ich kenne München **nicht gut**.
Regnet es?	–	**Ja**, es regnet.
	–	**Nein**, es regnet **nicht**.

- *nicht* is placed in front of the part of sentence that is being negated: *nicht gut, nicht schön, nicht Herr Heinrich.*
- When a whole sentence is negated, *nicht* is placed at the end: *Nein, es regnet nicht.*

12 *What adjectives do you know now? Write them down from memory.*

_____

_____

13 *Simply say* NEIN.

Das Hotel ist prima.	–	Nein, das Hotel ist nicht prima.
Das Wetter ist schön.	–	Nein, _____
Es regnet.	–	Nein, _____
Das Zentrum ist weit.	–	_____
Das Hotel ist praktisch.	–	_____
Die Reise ist prima.	–	_____

14 *Revision*
Note these expressions. It would be best to learn them by heart.

Asking how someone is

Guten Tag, Frau / Herr + Nachname	*Hello / Good morning / afternoon, Frau / Herr + surname*
Guten Morgen, Frau / Herr + Nachname	*Good morning, Frau / Herr + surname*
Guten Abend, Frau / Herr + Nachname	*Good evening, Frau / Herr + surname*
Wie geht's?	*How are you? (informal)*
Wie geht es Ihnen?	*How are you? (formal)*
Danke, sehr gut / gut / nicht schlecht / es geht.	*Very well / Fine / Not bad / OK, thank you.*
Danke, nicht so gut.	*Thanks for asking, not so good.*

Small talk: Travel and weather

Wie war die Reise?	*How was the journey / your trip?*
– Danke, gut.	*– Fine, thanks.*
Wie ist das Wetter? –	*What's the weather like? –*
Es regnet. / Es ist nicht so schön. /	*It's raining. / It's not so nice. /*
Es ist schön / warm / kalt.	*It's nice / fine / warm / cold.*
Das Wetter ist prima / gut / sehr gut / schön / schlecht.	*The weather's great / good / very good / nice / fine / bad.*
Die Sonne scheint.	*The sun is shining.*
Es schneit.	*It's snowing.*
Es ist windig.	*It's windy.*

15 *Listen and repeat.*

Tag	Guten Tag.	schön	Es ist schön.
Wie	Wie geht's?	schlecht	Es ist schlecht.
Wetter	Wie ist das Wetter?	windig	Es ist windig.
Sonne	Die Sonne scheint.	schneien	Es schneit.

16 *Add sehr. First listen, then repeat.*

schön	sehr schön	weit	sehr weit
gut	sehr gut	warm	sehr warm
schlecht	sehr schlecht	kalt	sehr kalt

17 *Supply the article, and then repeat.*

_____ Name   _____ Adresse

_____ Land   _____ Geburtsland

_____ Familienstand   _____ Nationalität

18 *Listen to the names of countries.*

Brasilien	Frankreich	Österreich
China	Italien	Russland
Deutschland	Korea	Türkei
England	Neuseeland	

19 *Listen and read at the same time.*
Look up exercise 5 (Textbook page 18).

Cultural info (Textbook page 20)

Before you do the test, open the textbook. Do you recognize the countries at first sight?

Supply the names of countries and find all the names that end in -land. How many are there?
Do you recognize the country? Match the country names.

Vocabulary

1. Mark the correct translation.

1. Wie geht's?
☐ Where are you from?
☐ How are you?
☐ What's the weather like?

2. Sehr gut.
☐ Very badly.
☐ Very well.
☐ Not very well.

3. Leider schlecht.
☐ Great.
☐ You're lucky.
☐ Bad, I'm afraid.

2. What's the weather like? Please match.

◯ Es ist sehr warm.

◯ Es ist windig.

◯ Es ist kalt.

◯ Die Sonne scheint.

◯ Es regnet.

◯ Es schneit.

1

2

3

4

5

6

Grammar

3. Supply the article.

1. _____ Name

2. _____ Stadt

3. _____ Land

4. _____ Adresse

5. _____ Hotel

6. _____ Zentrum

4. What is positive? Mark with a cross.

1. ☐ Das Wetter ist schön.
2. ☐ Ich kenne die Stadt nicht gut.
3. ☐ Das Hotel ist nicht weit.
4. ☐ Das ist sehr praktisch.

5. ☐ Sie haben Glück.
6. ☐ Es regnet schon zwei Tage.
7. ☐ Das Wetter ist nicht schön.
8. ☐ Aber die Reise ist prima.

5. Please negate.

1. Das ist weit.   Nein, _____.

2. Das ist schön.   _____.

3. Es ist kalt.   _____.

4. Es ist windig.   _____.

5. Es regnet.   _____.

6. Es schneit.   _____.

Check your answers in the key at the back of the book and then add up your points.

Total:

1 – 15	Before you carry on, you really should do this unit again.
16 – 25	Quite good, but not perfect yet. Please go over the dialogues and the grammar again. It'll be worth it.
26 – 29	Very good. You can carry straight on.

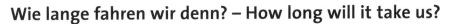
Wie lange fahren wir denn? – How long will it take us?

Claudia and Robert take the S-Bahn to Claudia's place. Claudia shares a flat with her friend Niki Bat in the north of Berlin.

Here are a lot of different questions that all start with a W-question word. This will also give you a chance to learn how to thank somebody, and some colloquial expressions that you can use in many different situations.

1 *Who says it?*
Please do exercise 1 as preparation. These are common responses in everyday speech. Note the gestures and head movement.

Aha, ich verstehe.	*Ah, I understand.*
Na ja, das ist nicht schlimm.	*Never mind.*

2 Claudia and Robert take the S-Bahn

5A

→ *First listen to the dialogue 5A at least twice.*
→ *Read the dialogue in the textbook.*
→ *Listen to the text and read the dialogue at the same time.*
→ *Now underline the stressed syllables.*
→ *Then read the dialogue following your underlinings.*
→ *Then turn to the vocabulary section. Try to learn the meaning of the words and the sentences by heart.*

Was kostet …?	*What does … cost? How much is …?*
kosten – er/sie kostet	*cost*
Fahrkarte (die), die Fahrkarten	*ticket*
zwei Euro	*two euros*
Euro (der), die Euro(s)	*euro*
Das habe ich.	*I've got that.*
Wo ist der Automat?	*Where is the ticket machine?*
Automat (der), die Automaten	*(ticket) machine*
Ich mache das.	*I'll do it.*
nett	*kind, nice*
Vielen Dank.	*Thank you very much.*
Wie lange fahren wir denn?	*How long does it take?*
fahren – er/sie fährt	*go, drive*
Stunde (die), die Stunden	*hour*
Wie bitte?	*Sorry?*
Minute (die), die Minuten	*minute*
Großstadt (die) (groß + die Stadt)	*city (groß = big)*
Kleinstadt (die) (klein + die Stadt)	*small town (klein = small)*

Compound nouns sometimes consist of an adjective and a noun:
groß + die Stadt = die Großstadt.

5B

→ *Listen to part 5B.*
→ *Read the dialogue in the textbook.*
→ *Listen to the text and read the dialogue at the same time.*
→ *Underline the stressed syllables.*
→ *Read the dialogue following the stress marks.*
→ *Then turn to the vocabulary section.*

Morgen haben wir das Auto.	*We'll have the car tomorrow.*
Auto (das), die Autos	*car*
mit der S-Bahn	*by S-Bahn*
S-Bahn (die), die S-Bahnen	*S-Bahn (city and suburban railway)*
Wann kommt Niki denn nach Hause?	*When does Niki get home?*
Wann?	*When?*
nach Hause	*home*
Heute kommt er spät.	*He's coming late today.*
heute / spät	*today / late*
Er arbeitet wieder furchtbar viel.	*He's working terribly hard again.*
arbeiten – er / sie arbeitet	*work*
wieder	*again*
furchtbar viel / wenig	*terribly much, hard / little*
Hast du ein Glück!	*You're lucky!*

3 *Read the text and fill in the right question word. Do you still remember which it is? Listen to the dialogue again and check your answers.*

4 *That's wrong!*
Write the correct sentence.

5 Wie bitte? *Read and complete.*
Two people are having problems communicating. The complete sentence is not so elegant, but clearer.
Now listen and compare.

6 *A few questions. – Give a brief answer. Write.*
When you give an answer, you can do it in a short sentence or a long one. Read the question and the long sentence. Then find the matching short answer. The short version is used in everyday speech.

7 *Write the singular.*

30

New Verbs – Neue Verben

		haben	arbeiten	fahren
Singular	ich	habe	arbeite	fahre
	du	**hast**	arbeit**est**	f**ä**hrst
	er/sie/es	**hat**	arbeit**et**	f**ä**hrt
Plural	wir	haben	arbeiten	fahren
	ihr	habt	arbeitet	fahrt
	sie/Sie	haben	arbeiten	fahren

The verb has a different ending for each person, but some verbs change the stem, too, in the second and third person:

- *hast* and *hat* are irregular.
- *a* becomes *ä*: *fahren – du fährst, er/sie/es fährt.*
- After a *-t* or *-d* an extra *-e-* is inserted. This makes pronunciation easier: du *arbeitest, er arbeitet / du findest, er findet.*

8 *All the special forms are missing in the following table. Fill them in.*

		haben	arbeiten	fahren
Singular	ich	habe	arbeite	fahre
	du			
	er / sie / es			
Plural	wir	haben	arbeiten	fahren
	ihr	habt		fahrt
	sie/Sie	haben	arbeiten	fahren

9 *Match the right article.*

_____ Minute   _____ Großstadt   _____ Kleinstadt   _____ S-Bahn

_____ Fahrkarte   _____ Euro   _____ Stunde   _____ Auto

Nomen im Plural – Nouns in the plural

Singular	Plural
der Tag	die Tag**e**
das Jahr	die Jahr**e**
die Stadt	die St**ä**dt**e**
das Land	die L**ä**nd**er**
das Wort	die W**ö**rt**er**
der Name	die Name**n**
die Fahrkarte	die Fahrkarte**n**
die Minute	die Minute**n**

Note: *die* = feminine singular (**die** Minute) and plural (der Tag, **die** Tage / die Minute, **die** Minuten / das Jahr, **die** Jahre)

10 *What are they? Write the answers.*

1 Das sind zwei _____

2 fünf _____

3 drei _____

4 drei _____

5 zwei _____

6 zwei _____

1

6 Name
   Adresse

Polen

Spanien

5

2

3

4 Markus Graf
   Steffi Sommer
   Toni Koch

11 *Please complete.*
For example: ein Jahr *– drei* Jahre

_____ Minute   – drei _____   _____ Kleinstadt – drei _____

_____ Stunde   – drei _____   _____ Geschäft – drei _____

_____ Stadt   – drei _____   _____ S-Bahn   – drei _____

_____ Großstadt – drei _____   _____ Auto   – drei _____

The number one: - We count *eins – zwei – drei – vier* etc.
- *ein-* changes when used in combination with a noun: *ein Tag (der Tag) – zwei Tage;*
eine Stunde (die Stunde) – zwei Stunden; ein Wort (das Wort) – zwei Wörter

12 *Revision*
Note these expressions. It would be best to learn them by heart.

Thanking

Danke./Vielen Dank. – Bitte.	*Thank you./Thank you very much. – That's OK./* *You're welcome./Not at all./Don't mention it.*
Das ist nett (von dir).	*That's nice/kind (of you). (informal)*
Das ist nett (von Ihnen).	*That's nice/kind (of you). (formal)*

Colloquial expressions

(Das ist) super. (Das ist) prima.	*(That's) super. (That's) great.*
Furchtbar viel/wenig/alt/schlecht.	*Terribly hard, much/little/old/bad.*
Wie bitte?	*Sorry?*

Furchtbar viel *is* sehr sehr viel.
You can also say: furchtbar lange *or* furchtbar alt …

13 a or ä, o or ö. Fill in and then repeat.

die St__ dt   –   die St__ dte

das L__ nd   –   die L__ nder

das W__ rt   –   die W__ rter

der S__ tz   –   die S__ tze

der P__ ss   –   die P__ sse

14A Who is that man?

→ Listen to the dialogue.

→ Complete the following text.

Herr Binder arbeitet i__ B__ __ __ __ __ .

Er ist s__ __ __ __ ein J__ __ __ dort.

Er k__ __ __ __ Frau Antes.

14B

→ And now repeat. Try to imitate the speaker's stress and pronunciation as closely as possible. This is naturally spoken everyday speech.

→ If you're not sure whether you've understood everything, you can read the text here:

Frau Antes:	Wer ist der Herr da?
Herr Meyer:	Das ist Herr Binder. Er arbeitet jetzt in Bremen.
Frau Antes:	Hallo, Herr Binder! Was machen Sie denn hier?
Herr Binder:	Ja Frau Antes, guten Tag. Wie geht's Ihnen denn?
Frau Antes:	Danke, gut. Und Ihnen?
Herr Binder:	Auch gut.
Frau Antes:	Sind Sie schon lange hier?
Herr Binder:	Ja, schon ein Jahr.

Cultural info (Textbook p. 24)

Germany is at the heart of Europe. It has nine neighbouring countries. There is access to the sea in the north, to the North Sea and Baltic Sea.

Which countries are they?
Listen to the country names. Note down the answers.

Write the country names on the map.

Vocabulary

1. Mark the correct translation.

1. Danke.
☐ Please.
☐ Thank you.
☐ Sorry.

2. Was kostet das?
☐ How much is it?
☐ When do you get home?
☐ How long does it take?

3. nach Hause
☐ to work
☐ from work
☐ home

4. wenig Zeit
☐ little time
☐ a lot of time
☐ one hour

5. furchtbar viel
☐ terribly little
☐ terribly hard
☐ very small

6. Wie bitte?
☐ How do I ask?
☐ Sorry?
☐ Who is it, please?

2. Write the singular.

1. die Städte _____

2. fünf Minuten eine _____

3. zehn Stunden eine _____

4. die Fahrkarten _____

5. die Wörter _____

6. zwei Länder ein _____

Grammar

3. Fill in the verb.

1. _____ du zu Hause? (arbeiten)

2. _____ du heute Zeit? (haben)

3. Wir _____ sehr viel. (arbeiten)

4. _____ ihr mit dem Auto? (fahren)

5. Wir _____ mit der S-Bahn. (fahren)

6. Was _____ die Fahrkarte? (kosten)

4. Supply the article.

1. _____ Wörter

2. _____ S-Bahn

3. _____ Fahrkarten

4. _____ Automat

5. _____ Großstadt

6. _____ Auto

Which words are plural? Note down the numbers: _____ .

5. Fill in a, ä, o or ö.

1. die St__ dt

2. die W__ rter

3. die S__ tze

4. das L__ nd

5. der P__ ss

6. die P__ sse

Check your answers in the key at the back of the book and then add up your points.

Total:	1 – 15	It would be a good idea to do this unit again straightaway.
	16 – 26	Pretty good. But it wouldn't hurt to go over the dialogues and the grammar again.
	27 – 30	Excellent. If you like, you could go over the vocabulary again, otherwise you can carry straight on.

Wer ist Claudia? Wer ist Robert? – Who is ...?

Now it really is time to find out a bit more about Claudia and Robert. You want to get to know them a bit better, don't you?

You will learn how to make statements about people and ask the corresponding questions. There is a lot about numbers and figures. And at the end we'll introduce you to a special sight.

1 *Who is who? Please match.*
What do you think the people look like? Please match. You know some of them, but not yet others. If you don't know all the words, please look them up in the glossary at the back of the workbook.

2   Claudia and Robert

→ *Listen to the text 6A at least twice.*
→ *Read the text in the textbook.*
→ *Listen and read the text at the same time.*
→ *Underline the stressed syllables.*
→ *Read the text following your underlinings.*
→ *Then turn to the vocabulary section. Try to learn the meaning of the words and the sentences by heart.*

6A

Claudia ist in Berlin geboren.	*Claudia was born in Berlin.*
Sie ist 23 Jahre alt.	*She is 23 years old.*
Sie ist Medien-Designerin von Beruf.	*She works as a media designer.*
Sie ist ... (Designerin / Stewardess) von Beruf.	*She works as a ... (designer / flight attendant).*
Beruf (der), die Berufe	*job, profession*
Sie arbeitet bei ...	*She works for ...*
Ihre Hobbys sind Reisen und Sprachen.	*Her hobbies are travel and languages.*
Hobby (das), die Hobbys	*hobby*
Sprache (die), die Sprachen	*language*
Ihre Handy-Nummer ist ...	*Her mobile (phone) number is ...*
Handy-Nummer (die), die Handy-Nummern	*mobile (phone) number*

6B

→ *Listen to part 6B.*
→ *Read the text in the textbook.*
→ *Listen and read the text at the same time.*
→ *Underline the stressed syllables.*
→ *Then turn to the vocabulary section.*

eine Kleinstadt in Bayern	*a small town in Bavaria*
Sie liegt südlich von München.	*It is situated south of Munich.*
liegen – er / sie liegt	*lie, be situated/located*
südlich von	*south of*
Robert studiert Informatik.	*Robert is studying computer science.*
studieren – er / sie studiert	*study*
Student (der), -en / die Studentin, -nen	*student*
Er hat viele Hobbys und immer	*He has a lot of hobbies and always*
wenig Zeit.	*little time.*
immer	*always*
Seine Handy-Nummer ist …	*His mobile (phone) number is …*
Seine Telefonnummer ist …	*His telephone number is …*
Telefonnummer (die), -n	*telephone number*
(das Telefon + die Nummer)	
Er findet Claudia sehr sympathisch.	*He likes Claudia a lot.*
sympathisch	*nice*

Er studiert **X** Informatik.
Sie studiert **X** Sprachen.
Nanni Köhler ist **X** Ärztin.
X = no article.

3 *Where does Robert come from? Where is he studying? Where is he now?*
Complete the sentences.

4 *What's missing?*

5 *We ask – you answer*
Write complete sentences.

6 *What do you think of it?*
Match the sentences to the drawings.

7 *Sorry? Ask questions as in the example.*
You are having a conversation, but you don't understand everything and have to ask a question to check. Listen to the sentence and ask. Then listen to the right question.

8 *What do you think of them? Fill in the person and the adjective.*
Have you already formed an impression of the people you've met so far?

wh-questions – W-Fragen

Wer ist Claudia?   **Wie** alt ist sie?
Woher kommt sie?   **Was** ist sie von Beruf?
Wo wohnt sie?   **Wie** lange kennt sie Robert?

- Question words begin with a *W.*
- Be careful with *wer* and *wo.* They look like „where" and „who" – but it's exactly the other way round: *wer?* = who? ↔ *wo?* = where?
- wh-questions usually include *denn.* This makes them sound more personal:
  Wer ist *denn* Claudia? Woher kommt sie *denn*? Wo wohnt sie *denn*?

9 *You are a bit curious and would like to find out a bit more about Robert. Find the matching answer.*

1. Wie heißt Robert denn mit Nachnamen?   a. Nein, nicht so viel.
2. Wo wohnt er denn?   b. Sehr sympathisch.
3. Wo liegt denn Bayern?   c. Er heißt Klein.
4. Wo studiert er?   d. Er studiert Informatik.
5. Was studiert er denn?   e. In Rosenheim in Bayern.
6. Arbeitet Robert viel?   f. Im Süden von Deutschland.
7. Wie findet er Claudia?   g. In München.

Numbers – Zahlen

1|47

You learned numbers 0 to 10 in lesson 3.

10 **zehn**	17 **sieb**zehn	30 dreiß**ig**	200 zwei**hundert**
11 **elf**	18 acht**zehn**	40 vier**zig**	300 drei**hundert**
12 **zwölf**	19 neun**zehn**	50 fünf**zig**	400 vier**hundert**
13 drei**zehn**		60 sech**zig**	500 fünf**hundert**
14 vier**zehn**	20 zwan**zig**	70 sieb**zig**	600 sechs**hundert**
15 fünf**zehn**	21 **einundzwanzig**	80 acht**zig**	700 sieben**hundert**
16 **sechzehn**	22 **zweiundzwanzig**	90 neun**zig**	800 acht**hundert**
	…		900 neun**hundert**
		100 **hundert**	
		101 hundert**eins**	1000 **tausend**
		102 hundert**zwei**	2000 zwei**tausend**
		…	1000 000 **eine Million**

Read numbers 13-99 – with the exception of the tens – from right to left:
13 = *dreizehn*, 21 = *einundzwanzig.*

10 *Write the numbers out in full.*

150 Euro	_____ Euro	15 Euro	_____ Euro
25 Euro	_____ Euro	5 Euro	_____ Euro
73 Euro	_____ Euro	99 Euro	_____ Euro

11 *Listen and note down the missing numbers.*

1. 089 – __ __ 37 49.   Das ist in München.

2. 040 – 77 8__ 90.   Das ist in Hamburg.

3. 030 – 30__ 26 5__ .   Das ist in Berlin.

4. 069 – __ 2 __ 6 __ 0.   Das ist in Frankfurt am Main.

Phone numbers consist of a dialling code, e.g. 089 for Munich or 030 for Berlin, and the personal phone number. The numbers are usually spoken individually as in English, so you say, for example, 3 – 4 – 6 – 5 – 8 – 3.

12 *Revision*
Note these expressions. It would be best to learn them by heart.

Asking about Places & Countries

Wo liegt … (+ Ort/Stadt/Land)?	*Where is … (+ place/city/country)?*
Im Norden/Süden/Osten/Westen von …	*In the north/south/east/west of …*
Nördlich/Südlich/Östlich/Westlich von …	*North/South/East/West of …*

Personal Questions

Wie heißen Sie? – (Ich heiße …) … (Vorname + Zuname)	*What's your name? – My name is … (first name + surname)*
Wie ist Ihr Name? – … Ich buchstabiere.	*What's your name? – … I'll spell it.*
Woher sind Sie? – Aus …	*Where are you from? – From …*
Wo arbeiten Sie?	*Where do you work?*
– Bei … (Firmenname)	*– For … (company name)*
Wo sind Sie geboren? –	*Where were you born?*
– In … (Land/Stadt/Ort)	*– In … (country/city/place)*
Wo wohnen Sie? – In … (Stadt/Ort)	*Where do you live? – In … (city/place)*
Wie alt sind Sie? – Ich bin … (24) Jahre alt.	*How old are you? – I'm … (24) years old.*
Was sind Sie von Beruf?	*What do you do?*
– Ich bin … (Designerin/Ingenieur)	*– I'm a … (designer/engineer)*
Wie ist Ihre Adresse?	*What's your address?*
Wie heißt du?	*What's your name?*
Woher bist du?	*Where are you from?*
Was studierst du?	*What are you studying?*

13 *Repeat these numbers.*

zwei	zwanzig	zweihundert
drei	dreißig	dreihundert
vier	vierzig	vierhundert
fünf	fünfzig	fünfhundert
sechs	sechzig	sechshundert
sieben	siebzig	siebenhundert

14 *I'll spell it.*

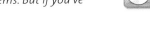

If you've got an easy name, you're lucky and don't have a lot of problems. But if you've got a complicated one, you often have to spell it.
Spell your name and say your phone number.
Start with: Ich heiße … Ich buchstabiere: … Meine Telefonnummer ist: …

Here's the alphabet for spelling something over the phone:

A wie Anton	**J** wie Julius	**S** wie Samuel
B wie Berta	**K** wie Kaufmann	**T** wie Theodor
C wie Cäsar	**L** wie Ludwig	**U** wie Ulrich
D wie Dora	**M** wie Martha	**V** wie Viktor
E wie Emil	**N** wie Nordpol	**W** wie Wilhelm
F wie Friedrich	**O** wie Otto	**X** wie Xanthippe
G wie Gustav	**P** wie Paula	**Y** wie Ypsilon
H wie Heinrich	**Q** wie Quelle	**Z** wie Zacharias
I wie Ida	**R** wie Richard	

Cultural info Neuschwanstein (Textbook, page 28)

Southern Germany is a tourist centre. No federal state has as many tourists as Bavaria and Munich, and the numbers are rising all the time. Bavaria is the most popular holiday area among both Germans and tourists from all over the world.
The castles built by the Bavarian King Ludwig II in the 19th century are just an hour's drive from Munich. He was the fairytale king who loved castles and music, especially Wagner, whom he brought to Munich. The fact that the king, towards the end of his life, was a very lonely figure, and that he died rather mysteriously in Lake Starnberg means he is shrouded with a fairytale cloak of magic and mystery.

Answer the questions.

1. *Write the word or words.*

1. K _ ei _ st _ dt

2. v_ _ l_ n D_ _ k

3. T_ _ _ fonnum_ _ _

4. n_ _ _ Hau_ _

5. Ho_ _ y

6. i_ t_ ress_ _ _

2. *Write the sentences.*

1. erstudiert _____

2. siestudiertinhamburg _____

3. eristindeutschlandgeboren _____

4. eristdreijahrealt _____

5. woarbeitensie _____

6. wassindsievonberuf _____

3. *Underline the right form.*

1. Wo [arbeiten] [arbeitest] [arbeite] du?

2. Wer [studieren] [studiert] [studiere] Informatik?

3. Ich [fahre] [fährst] [fahren] immer mit der S-Bahn.

4. Wann [kommst] [kommt] [kommen] du nach Hause?

5. Wann [habe] [hast] [hat] du Zeit?

4. *Here are some important questions that you're bound to be able to use in a conversation. Underline the right question word.*

1. [Wer] [Wo] [Was] sind Sie geboren?

2. [Was] [Wer] [Wie lange] sind Sie von Beruf?

3. [Wie] [Wie lange] [Wo] arbeiten Sie? (Firma)

4. [Was] [Wie] [Wo] finden Sie die Arbeit?

5. [Wie] [Wie lange] [Wo] arbeiten Sie schon dort?

6. [Wer] [Wie] [Was] sind Ihre Hobbys?

(1|51)

5. *Listen to the short dialogue and mark the right answers.*

1. Der Mann
☐ ist in Deutschland geboren.
☐ ist nicht in Deutschland geboren.

2. Er
☐ arbeitet.
☐ studiert.

3. Er ist
☐ ein Jahr da.
☐ schon fünf Jahre da.

Check your answers in the key at the back of the book and then add up your points.

Total: | 1 – 14 Oh dear, it's a pity. Please do this unit again.

15 – 23 Not so bad. But even so, it would be a good idea to go over the dialogues and the grammar again.

24 – 26 Excellent. There's nothing to stop you carrying on.

Entschuldigung! – Sorry!

Before getting down to work, Herr Heinrich offers his guest something to drink.
In this dialogue you learn how to express a wish and how to ask somebody what they
wish to have. The modal verbs *möchten* and *können* play an important part.

1 *Please complete.*
Please do exercise 1 as preparation.
The question you use when you ask someobody what they wish to have is Möchten
Sie ... / Möchtest du ...? – Would you like ...? *If you don't know all the words, please
look them up in the glossary.*

2 **Drinking coffee in the office**
→ *First listen to what Herr Heinrich and Frau Bruckner say. Something seems to have
    happened. Listen to the conversation at least twice.*
→ *Read the dialogue.*
→ *Listen and read at the same time. If you like, you can underline the stressed syllables.*
→ *Now learn the vocabulary.*

Möchten Sie etwas trinken?	*Would you like something to drink?*
möchten – er / sie möchte	*would like*
etwas	*something*
trinken – er / sie trinkt	*drink*
Kaffee (der)	*coffee*
Haben Sie auch Tee?	*Do you have tea, too?*
Tee (der)	*tea*
Ja, natürlich.	*Yes, of course.*
tut mir Leid	*sorry*
Der Tee ist schon kalt.	*The tea is (already) cold.*
Dann nehme ich Kaffee.	*Then I'll take coffee.*
Milch (die)	*milk*
Zucker (der)	*sugar*
Nur Milch, bitte.	*Just milk, please.*
nur	*just, only*
Macht nichts.	*That's OK. Never mind.*
	[literally: it makes nothing]
nichts	*nothing*
Hier ist eine Serviette.	*Here is a serviette.*
Serviette (die), die Servietten	*serviette, napkin*
Wir arbeiten jetzt bis Mittag.	*We'll work now till lunchtime / midday.*
Mittag (der), die Mittage	*lunchtime, midday*
Dann machen wir eine Stunde Pause	*Then we'll take an hour's break*
Pause (die), die Pausen	*break*

und gehen in die Kantine.	and go to the canteen.
gehen – er / sie geht	go
Kantine (die), die Kantinen	canteen
Einverstanden.	OK. Fine.

Do you know now what happened? Herr Heinrich spilt some coffee, but luckily only into the saucer. That's why he's bringing a napkin.

3 *What is the right order? Note down the numbers.*

4 *You ask.*
How does the sentence continue? Find the most suitable continuation. Note down the letters.

We say *Entschuldigung*:
• when we've had a mishap (= sorry)
• or when we make a polite request (= excuse me): *Entschuldigung, wie ist Ihr Name?*

5 *Crossword*
Can you do the crossword? Senkrecht *means Down,* waagerecht *means Across.*
Now find the solution – a word that you need all the time.
Take:
1. the fourth letter
2. the fifth letter
3. the fourth letter
4. the first letter
5. the third letter.   _ _ _ _ _

6 *Listen to the question. Answer politely. Then listen to the answer.*
You are the guest and are being asked what you would like. Select a polite response from the suggestions given.

7 *What doesn't fit?*
Write down the word that doesn't fit the group.

8 *Chris Bruckner's note*
Notes from the first day of the visit.

Articles: definite and indefinite – Artikel: bestimmt und unbestimmt:
der, die, das und *ein/eine*

Singular	masculine	feminine	neuter
personal pronoun	er	sie	es
definite article	der Name	die Adresse	das Land
indefinite article	**ein** Name	**eine** Adresse	**ein** Land

The definite article has three different forms, the indefinite article has two: *der/die/das* and *ein/eine*.

Careful: indefinite amounts don't need an article, or a word corresponding to English "some": *Möchten Sie Kaffee?/Tee, bitte, mit Milch.*

9 *Fill in the indefinite article (*ein/eine*).*

Was ist das?

Wasserburg	Das ist _____ Kleinstadt.
0170 – 82 73 47	Das ist _____ Handy-Nummer.
Andy	Das ist _____ Vorname.
Lettland	Das ist _____ Land in Nordeuropa.
81825	Das ist _____ Postleitzahl.
etwas	Das ist _____ Wort.

Verbs – Verben: e → *i(e)/möchten/können*

		nehmen	**möchten**	**können**
Singular	ich	nehme	möchte	**kann**
	du	nimmst	möchtest	**kannst**
	er/sie	nimmt	möchte	**kann**
Plural	wir	nehmen	möchten	können
	ihr	nehmt	möchtet	könnt
	sie/Sie	nehmen	möchten	können

- Some strong verbs change: *e* to *i* or *ie* (*nehmen: du nimmst, er/sie nimmt; lesen: du liest, er/sie liest, sprechen: du sprichst, er/sie spricht; geben: es gibt*)
- *möchten* expresses a wish. It's a modal verb: *Ich **möchte** noch etwas Kaffee.*
- *können* is also a modal verb. It is used to express a wish in the form of a question: ***Kann** ich bitte die Milch **haben**?*

When you use *möchten*, you are expressing yourself politely. So you can omit additional terms of politeness such as *bitte* or *gern*. Example: *Möchten Sie Kaffee oder Tee?*

10 *Which form is missing?*

| möchtet | kannst | kann | möchte | können | nimmt | kann | nimmst | möchtest |

		nehmen	möchten	können
Singular	ich	nehme		
	du			
	er/sie		möchte	
Plural	wir	nehmen	möchten	können
	ihr	nehmt		könnt
	sie/Sie	nehmen	möchten	

11 *Fill in* möchten *or* können.

_____ Sie Kaffee oder Tee?

_____ ich etwas Milch haben?

_____ ich eine Serviette haben?

_____ Sie telefonieren?

_____ ich bitte telefonieren? *(make a phone call)*

_____ Sie ein Hotelzimmer? *(hotel room)*

_____ Sie das wiederholen? *(repeat)*

_____ Sie mir helfen? *(help)*

12 *Fill in:* wer * wann * wo * wie * was * woher.

Können Sie mir sagen, … *(Could you tell me …)*

_____ das Hotel ist?   _____ die Fahrkarte kostet?

_____ der Bus kommt?   _____ Herr Bünzli kommt? Aus der Schweiz?

_____ der Herr heißt?   _____ Herr Heinrich ist?

13 *Revision*

Apologizing

Tut mir leid.	*Sorry.*
Entschuldigung.	*Sorry/Excuse me.*
Entschuldige/Entschuldigen Sie.	*Sorry/Excuse me. (informal/formal)*
(Das) macht nichts./Bitte.	*(That's) OK/all right./Never mind.*

Asking what someone would like / Offering

Möchten Sie …/Möchtest du … (Kaffee)?	*Would you like … (coffee)?*

14 *Mark with a cross.*
The vowels a, e, i, o, u can be either short or long in German. The difference is very important
for a good pronunciation. So try and imitate the speaker's pronunciation as exactly as possible.
Listen and mark with a cross whether the vowels are long or short, then repeat.

	kurz (short)	lang (long)		kurz (short)	lang (long)
haben	☐	☐	schlecht	☐	☐
hat	☐	☐	schon	☐	☐
da	☐	☐	kommt	☐	☐
dann	☐	☐	Sie	☐	☐
Stadt	☐	☐	sind	☐	☐
Jahr	☐	☐	nur	☐	☐
Tee	☐	☐	eine Stunde	☐	☐

15 *Link the English expressions to the German equivalents. Listen, then read out loud.*

1|55

Who is that please?
This is (Meier/Beate Meier).

Ist dort Meier?
Nein, hier ist Keller.
Haben Sie 34 57?

Is that Meier?
Speaking. / Yes, this is Meier.

Nein, 34 77.
Entschuldigung. Auf Wiederhören.

Is that Meier?
No, this is Keller.
Is your number 34 57?
No, 34 77.
Goodbye.

Wer ist dort bitte?
Hier ist Meier. / Hier ist Beate Meier.

Ist dort Meier?
Ja, hier Meier.

Cultural info (Textbook, page 32)

You can be taken by surprise in a café. In Germany espresso and cappuccino from Italy
are popular drinks alongside coffee with milk. There's nowhere that has so many different sorts of coffee as Austria. There's black coffee (black without milk or sugar), brown
coffee (black coffee with whipped cream), a "Kapuziner" (small black coffee with whipped cream), mocca (strong black coffee, mocca is an Arabic word), a double mocca
(double portion of mocca), "Melange" (made of equal portions of coffee and milk),
"Wiener Melange" (like Melange, but with foamy milk) and "Fiaker" (black coffee with
rum or cognac). Completely confusing if you're a stranger.
And it's not always so easy in Switzerland either. If you ask for a "Schale" (bowl), you'll
get a coffee with milk.

Vocabulary

1. Please complete.

1. Kaffee oder _____?

2. Tee mit Z_____

3. Entschuldigung. – Macht _____.

4. Mann und _____

5. Hobby und _____

6. im Norden und im S_____

2. What's right?

1. Macht nichts.
☐ That's OK.
☐ That's all I need.
☐ That's kind of you.

3. Ich möchte …
☐ I'd like …
☐ I take …
☐ I have …

5. Tut mir leid, …
☐ I'm fine.
☐ I'm sorry.
☐ That's OK.

2. Kann ich bitte …?
☐ I'll take …
☐ Can I please …?
☐ Do you have …?

4. Einverstanden?
☐ OK?
☐ How much?
☐ What would you like?

6. Ja, natürlich.
☐ OK, fine.
☐ Right.
☐ Yes, of course.

Grammar

3. Fill in.

1. Möchte____ Sie Tee?

2. Ich möcht____ gern Kaffee.

3. Ich nehm____ Zucker und Milch.

4. Wir arbeit____ bis Mittag.

5. Wer geh____ in die Kantine?

6. Mach____ Sie auch eine Pause?

7. Könn____ wir jetzt eine Pause machen?

8. Wer k_____ mir helfen?

4. Fill in ein / eine.

1. _____ Person

2. _____ Hotel

3. _____ Straße

4. _____ Übung

5. _____ Großstadt

6. _____ Ort

7. _____ Reise

8. _____ Hobby

Check your answers in the key at the back of the book and then add up your points.

Total:
1 – 16	Before you carry on, you should do this unit again.
17 – 23	Quite good, but not perfect yet. Please go over the dialogue and the grammar again.
24 – 28	Excellent. There's nothing to stop you carrying on.

Zu Hause – At home

Claudia and Robert have finally got home after an hour's journey. Claudia's friend Niki is already there.
Niki tells them what he has prepared. He talks about something in the past.
From here on you'll learn to talk about something that is over.

1 *There's something missing here. Please complete.*
*Do exercise 1 as preparation. All the vowels are missing. Does anything strike you? There are a lots of **e**s, especially in the endings:* hör**e**n, hör**e**, ess**e** *etc.*

2 At Claudia and Niki's place

→ *Now listen to how the story continues.*
→ *Read and listen.*
→ *Learn the words.*

Du bist ja zu Hause!	Oh, you're home.
zu Hause	(at) home
Na klar.	Yes, of course.
Ich bin extra früher gegangen.	I left early on purpose.
extra	on purpose, specially
früher	earlier
gehen – er/sie geht, ist gegangen	go, leave
Alles bestens.	Everything's just great.
Claudia sagt, du arbeitest viel.	Claudia says you work a lot.
sagen – er/sie sagt, hat gesagt	say
Ach was!	Not at all.
Von nichts kommt nichts. (Sprichwort)	Nothing comes of nothing. (proverb)
sagt man	people say
man	one, people, they
Die Arbeit macht auch Spaß.	Work is fun.
Spaß (der)	fun
Du hast recht.	You're right.
recht haben – er/sie hat recht	be right
Und jetzt essen wir was.	And now we'll have something to eat.
essen – du isst, er/sie isst, hat gegessen	eat
was = etwas	something
Nun bin ich dran.	Now it's my turn.
nun	now
dran sein – er/sie ist dran	be someone's turn
Ich habe nämlich eine Überraschung.	I have a surprise.
nämlich	namely, in fact
Überraschung (die), die Überraschungen	surprise

Es gibt heute Spaghetti und Salat.	*There's spaghetti and salad.*
geben – es gibt, hat gegeben	*give – there is/are*
Spaghetti (die Pl.)	*spaghetti [always plural]*
Salat (der), die Salate	*salad, lettuce*
Ich habe gekocht.	*I've cooked.*
kochen – er/sie kocht, hat gekocht	*cook*
klasse	*great*

3 *Please complete.*
Select the right expression. Then check your answers by listening to the text again.

4 *Jumbled letters.*
Find two words that are hidden in the puzzle. They are words you've already learned:

H_____ and D_____ .

5 *What do Robert, Niki and Claudia say? Mark the right answers.*
You remember what Robert, Claudia and Niki said, don't you?

6 *Please complete.*
The forms of sein *and* haben *are missing. They are part of the perfect tense used to talk about the past.*

7 *What do you say?*
Here you can check how good your reactions are. Reply with the appropriate expression.

8 *Robert's diary*

Perfect tense 1 – Das Perfekt 1

			kochen			gehen
Singular	ich	habe	**gekocht**	ich	bin	**gegangen**
	du	hast		du	bist	
	er / sie	hat		er / sie	ist	
Plural	wir	haben		wir	sind	
	ihr	habt		ihr	seid	
	sie / Sie	haben		sie / Sie	sind	

- When you talk about something in the past, you use the perfect.
  For example: *Gestern habe ich gekocht. Heute gehen wir essen.*
- The perfect is also possible in cases where you would use the simple past tense in English.
- The perfect consists of two parts: Gestern *habe* ich Spaghetti *gekocht*. You need the conjugated form of *haben* or *sein* (*ich habe, du hast* etc.) and the past participle (*gekocht*).
- The past participle usually starts with *ge-* and ends in *-(e)t* (*gearbeitet, gekocht*) or *-en* (*gegangen*). It is placed at the end of the sentence, and the form doesn't change.
- In German as in English there are weak and strong verbs. Weak ones have the ending *-(e)t*, strong ones *-en*.

9 *What is happening in the present? What happened in the past?*
*Mark with **G** (= Gegenwart = present) or **V** (= Vergangenheit = past).*

_____ Was hast du heute gemacht?   _____ Ich habe schon gegessen.

_____ Wo bist du geboren?   _____ Hast du gearbeitet?

_____ Fahrt ihr in die Stadt?   _____ Du hast recht.

_____ Was heißt das?   _____ Ich bin früh nach Hause gegangen.

_____ Hast du Hunger?   _____ Wohin fährt die Bahn?

Verbs with a vowel change – Verben mit Vokalwechsel

		fahren	**sprechen**	**lesen**
Singular	ich	fahre	spreche	lese
	du	fährst	sprichst	liest
	er / sie	fährt	spricht	liest
Plural	wir	fahren	sprechen	lesen
	ihr	fahrt	sprecht	lest
	sie / Sie	fahren	sprechen	lesen

Some strong verbs change the stem vowel: *a → ä, i → i(e)*.
du and *er/sie* forms that are special are given in the vocabulary lists.

10 *Note down the verbs with special* du *and* er / sie *forms.*

| lesen | machen | essen | haben | gehen |

| sein | geben | trinken | fahren | nehmen | sprechen |

Infinitiv	du	er / sie		Infinitiv	du	er / sie

11 *What's the opposite?*

etwas	nichts
jemand (somebody)	niemand *(nobody)*
viel	wenig
früher	später

Ich habe heute nichts gekocht.   Ich _____ .

Ist da jemand?   Da ist _____ _____ .

Du arbeitest zu wenig.   Nein, ich _____ .

Wir sind extra später gegangen.   Ich bin extra _____ .

12 *Revision*
Note the sentences. It would be best to learn them by heart.

Agreeing / Disagreeing

Du hast / Sie haben (nicht) recht.	You're (not) right.
Ja. / Nein. / Einverstanden.	Yes. / No. / OK / Fine.

Colloquial Expressions 2

Du bist ja zu Hause! – Na klar.	You're at home! – Of course.
Einverstanden? – Einverstanden.	OK? – OK.
(= Sind Sie / bist du einverstanden?	(= Are you in agreement?
– Ich bin einverstanden.)	– I am in agreement.)
was = etwas	something
extra: Ich bin extra früher gegangen.	specially: I left early, specially.
Das ist prima / klasse.	That's great.
Ich bin / Du bist / Sie sind dran.	It's my / your turn.

A lot of endings have an -e- in German. But this -e- is toned down and not spoken like a full -e-. The way you speak the endings is a good sign of how well you can already speak German.

13 *So listen carefully and repeat.*

essen	kochen	gehen
sagen	fragen	lesen
der Name	die Straße	die Adresse
die Tage	die Städte	die Berufe
der Hunger	das Wetter	die Nummer
die Studenten	die Minuten	die Verben

14 *Stress*
Here are a few perfect forms that you've already met. The stress is always on the second syllable. Try repeating them.

geboren   gemacht   gegessen   gearbeitet   gefahren   gegangen

15 *Write a dialogue. Complete the following seven sentences.*

Hallo.	Wer / … / dort / bitte?
Hier / Meyer.	… / dort Meyer / Telefon 46 88 11?
Nein / hier / … Meyer / Telefon 46 77 11.	Oh, Entschuldigung.
Bitte / sehr.	

Now listen and repeat.

Cultural info (Textbook page 36)

Proverbs and the images in them are a lot of fun. They're very typical of a language. Think about whether there's a similar proverb or saying in your language, and what image is used to express it.

Fill in the words.

To help you understand the proverbs here is a paraphrase or example.

If you take your time, you'll find a solution.
For example: The son who has turned out badly (= the apple) takes after his father (= the tree trunk).
It's often better to try something out than to think about it for a long time.
For example: If you are friendly (= the sound), you will get a friendly answer (= the music).
Someone who has a lot of worries comforts himself with a good vintage (= liqueur).

You'll find the translation in the glossary.

Vocabulary

1. *Please complete.*

| recht | was | Hunger | nichts | Spaß | dran |

1. Du hast _____. 4. Das macht _____.

2. Du bist _____. 5. Von nichts kommt _____.

3. Hast du _____? 6. Ach _____!

2. *Write the sentence.*

1. er | gegangen | extra | früher | ist   _____

2. arbeitet | er | viel   _____

3. recht | sie | hat   _____

4. eine | Überraschung | das | ist   _____

5. hat | wer | gekocht   _____

6. er | Spaghetti | hat | gekocht   _____

Grammar

3. *Fill in the forms of* haben *or* sein.

1. Was _____ du gekocht? (haben)

2. _____ Petra schon nach Hause gegangen? (sein)

3. _____ ihr in die Stadt gefahren? (sein)

4. Wir _____ um zwölf gegessen. (haben)

5. Er _____ viel gearbeitet. (haben)

6. Was _____ du heute gemacht? (haben)

4. *Write the 3rd person singular.*

1. fahren   er / sie _____

2. essen   er / sie _____

3. nehmen   er / sie _____

4. geben   es _____

5. sein   er / sie _____

6. sprechen   er / sie _____

Check your answers in the key at the back of the book and then add up your points.

Total:	1 – 12	It would be a good idea to do this unit again straightaway.
	13 – 20	Pretty good. But it wouldn't hurt to go over the dialogue and the grammar again.
	21 – 24	Excellent. If you like, you could go over the vocabulary again, otherwise you can carry straight on.

Die Wohnung ist schön – The flat is nice

Claudia and Niki only found their flat a short time ago. You'd probably like to find out
how they live.
As you do so, you'll find out quite a lot about flats, rents and adverts, and you'll be able
to say what you think of something. Adjectives of course have an important part of play
in all this.

1 *What is where?*
Please do exercise 1 as preparation.

das Wohnzimmer	*livingroom*
das Schlafzimmer	*bedroom*
die Küche	*kitchen*
das Bad	*bathroom*
die Toilette	*toilet*
der Flur	*hall(way)*
der Balkon	*balcony*

2 Two rooms, kitchen and bath

→ *Read the text.*
→ *If you need help with unknown words, have a look at the vocabulary list.*

Die Wohnung von Claudia und Niki ist nicht groß.	*Claudia and Niki's flat isn't big.*
Wohnung (die), die Wohnungen	*flat*
von	*of, from*
Sie ist aber sehr gemütlich.	*But it's very cosy.*
gemütlich	*cosy, comfortable*
Ein Zimmer mit Bad	*One room with a bath*
Zimmer (das), die Zimmer	*room*
Bad (das), die Bäder	*bath(room)*
das reicht, hat Niki immer gesagt.	*that's all I need, Niki always said.*
reichen – es reicht, hat gereicht	*be enough, be all you need*
sagen – er / sie sagt, hat gesagt	*say*
Und jetzt haben sie zwei Zimmer,	*And now they have two rooms,*
eine Küche und ein Bad.	*a kitchen and a bathroom.*
Küche (die), die Küchen	*kitchen*
Auch für Besuch ist Platz.	*There's room for visitors, too.*
für	*for*
Besuch (der)	*visit, visitor*
Platz (der)	*room, space*
Robert schläft im Wohnzimmer.	*Robert sleeps in the livingroom.*

53

schlafen – du schläfst, er / sie schläft, hat geschlafen	*sleep*
Claudia hat lange zu Hause gewohnt	*Claudia lived at home for a long time*
wohnen – er / sie wohnt, hat gewohnt	*live*
und die Miete gespart.	*and saved the rent.*
Miete (die), die Mieten	*rent*
sparen – er / sie spart, hat gespart	*save*
Dann haben sie die Wohnung im Norden von Berlin gefunden.	*Then they found a flat in the north of Berlin.*
finden – er / sie findet, hat gefunden	*find*
Claudia hat die Anzeige gelesen.	*Claudia read the advert.*
Anzeige (die), die Anzeigen	*ad, advert*
lesen – du liest, er / sie liest, hat gelesen	*read*
Dachwohnung (die), die Dachwohnungen	*penthouse*
45 qm (= Quadratmeter)	*45m² (= square metres)*
550 Euro monatlich, warm	*550 euros a month, including heating for*
ab sofort frei	*immediate occupation, available immediately*

You can listen to the text. Then read the text yourself out loud.

3 *What's right? Please mark the answer.*
You remember everything, don't you? Mark the correct statements.

4 *Now pretend you are Claudia talking about your flat. Say* ich *und* wir.

5 *Rents, rents, rents. Please match.*
Match the rents to the flats or houses. They are from the Munich area. Munich is the most expensive city in Germany.

6 *Some sums.*

7 *Fill in the verbs.*

8 *What do you think of this?*
First listen to the example. Then we'll ask and you reply. Listen to the correct solution.

sein *is followed by the nominative,* finden *by the accusative. A lot of verbs take the accusative.*

9 *Fill in the adjective.*
Adjectives to the left of a noun have an ending: das **schöne** Bad.
Adjectives to the right of a noun have no ending: Das Bad ist **schön**.

Perfect tense 2 – Das Perfekt 2

			kochen	wohnen	sparen	finden	lesen
Singular	ich	habe	gekocht	gewohnt	gespart	gefunden	gelesen
	du	hast					
	er/sie	hat					
Plural	wir	haben					
	ihr	habt					
	sie/Sie	haben					

In the text they talk about the past. There are some more perfect forms with *haben*.

10 *Note down the answer that fits.*

1. Wohnt er in Hamburg? _____
2. Spart sie? _____
3. Geht Peter nach Hause? _____
4. Findet Claudia eine Wohnung? _____
5. Liest sie die Anzeige? _____
6. Kochst du? _____

a. Sie hat gespart.
b. Er hat in Hamburg gewohnt.
c. Sie hat schon eine Wohnung gefunden.
d. Er ist schon nach Hause gegangen.
e. Sie hat die Anzeige schon gelesen.
f. Ich habe schon gekocht.

Articles: definite and indefinite – Artikel: bestimmt und unbestimmt –
Nominativ und Akkusativ: *der, ein – den, einen*

Singular		masculine		feminine		neuter	
definite article	*nom.*	der	Balkon	die	Küche	das	Bad
indefinite article		ein	Balkon	eine	Küche	ein	Bad
definite article	*acc.*	den	Balkon	die	Küche	das	Bad
indefinite article		einen	Balkon	eine	Küche	ein	Bad

11 *Fill in the indefinite article* (ein / eine).

Was ist das?

1. Das ist _____ Kantine.

2. Das ist _____ Bad.

3. Das ist _____ Wohnzimmer.

4. Das ist _____ Balkon.

5. Das ist _____ Küche.

6. Das ist _____ Schlafzimmer.

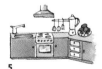

12 *Now fill in the definite article* (der/die/das).

_____ Kantine ist sehr groß.   _____ Balkon ist schön.

_____ Bad ist klein.   _____ Küche ist praktisch.

_____ Wohnzimmer ist gemütlich.   _____ Schlafzimmer ist nicht groß.

13 *Fill in the definite article* (den, die, das).

Wie finden Sie _____ Kantine?   Wie finden Sie _____ Balkon?

Wie finden Sie _____ Bad?   Wie finden Sie _____ Küche?

Wie finden Sie _____ Wohnzimmer?   Wie finden Sie _____ Schlafzimmer?

14 *Fill in the indefinite article* (einen, eine, ein).

Wir haben _____ Wohnung gefunden. Sie ist sehr schön.

Wir haben _____ Anzeige gelesen. Sie ist sehr interessant.

Wir haben _____ Lösung gefunden. Sie ist richtig.

Wir haben _____ Salat gemacht. Er ist sehr gut.

Wir haben _____ Büro im Zentrum gefunden. Das ist sehr praktisch.

15 *Some revision, and new words that belong to the topic.*

Living

wohnen – er / sie wohnt, hat gewohnt	*live*
die Wohnung, die Wohnungen	*flat, apartment*
das Haus, die Häuser	*house*
das Wohnzimmer	*livingroom*
das Schlafzimmer	*bedroom*
die Küche, die Küchen	*kitchen*
das Bad, die Bäder	*bathroom*
der Balkon, die Balkone	*balcony*
der Flur, die Flure	*hall(way)*
die Toilette, die Toiletten	*toilet*
die Terrasse, die Terrassen	*terrace/patio*
der Garten, die Gärten	*garden*
die Tür, die Türen	*door*
die Garage, die Garagen	*garage*
die 2-Zimmer-Wohnung	*two-room flat*
die Miete, die Mieten	*rent*
monatlich kalt / warm	*basic rent per month without/with heating etc.*
der Platz (viel / wenig Platz)	*room, space (lot of/litte room)*
gemütlich – alt – neu	*cosy, comfortable – old – new*

16 *Say the numbers. Imitate the speaker's pronunciation as precisely as you can.*
Pay special attention to z- and the ending -zig.

zehn	zwanzig	dreißig	siebzig
elf	einundzwanzig	vierzig	achtzig
zwölf	zweiundzwanzig	fünfzig	neunzig
dreizehn	dreiundzwanzig	sechzig	hundert
…	…		

17 *Now listen to a few prices. Note down the numbers.*

Kaffee: _____ €

Fahrkarte: _____ €

Wohnung: _____ €

Haus: _____ €

1-Zimmer-Wohnung München: _____ €

1-Zimmer-Wohnung Norddeutschland: _____ €

18 *Listen and repeat.*
A couple is looking for a flat. The husband is phoning the landlord.

Herr Bergmann:	Bergmann.
Paul Fischer:	Guten Tag, Herr Bergmann. Hier Fischer.
	Wir haben Ihre Anzeige gelesen.
	Ist die Wohnung noch frei?
Herr Bergmann:	Ja, da haben Sie Glück. Die ist noch frei.
Paul Fischer:	Prima. Wir – hm – meine Frau und ich – kommen sofort. Geht das?
Herr Bergmann:	Ja. Es ist jetzt 3 Uhr. Wann sind Sie dann hier?
Paul Fischer:	So um 5. Nicht später.
Herr Bergmann:	Gut, also dann bis 5.
Paul Fischer:	Bis 5. Vielen Dank. Auf Wiedersehen.

Cultural info (Textbook page 40)

The solution is something you can wish somebody, an expression you can use in many different situations. To go with it, there are some symbols of good luck.

Fill in the numbers.
Write the letters.

das Hufeisen	*horseshoe*
der Fliegenpilz	*fly agaric [toadstool]*
der Schornsteinfeger	*chimney sweep*
das Kleeblatt	*cloverleaf*

Vocabulary

1. Mark the correct translation.

1. die Wohnung
☐ flat
☐ hallway
☐ living room

2. die Anzeige
☐ advert
☐ time
☐ newspaper

3. die Garage
☐ garden
☐ garage
☐ patio

4. 500 € monatlich kalt
☐ 500 euros a month with heating
☐ 500 euros a month basic rent
☐ 500 euros a week

5. ab sofort frei
☐ available immediately
☐ available from the end of the month
☐ no deposit

6. Die Wohnung ist gemütlich.
☐ The flat is big.
☐ It's a nice flat.
☐ The flat is cosy.

Grammar

2. Fill in the article.

1. Die Wohnung hat 2 Zimmer: _____ Wohnzimmer und _____ Schlafzimmer.

2. Sie hat natürlich auch _____ Flur, _____ Küche und _____ Bad.

3. Sie hat k_____ Terrasse.

4. Aber sie hat _____ Balkon.

5. _____ Bad ist nicht sehr groß.

6. _____ Toilette ist extra.

3. Fill in: gewohnt, gefunden, gespart, gesagt, gelesen, gemietet.

1. Wir haben eine Wohnung _____ . (finden)

2. Was hast du _____ ?

3. Ich habe Geld _____ . Ich habe zu Hause _____ .

4. Wir haben die Anzeige _____ .

5. Wir haben eine Dachwohnung _____ . (mieten)

Listening Comprehension

2|6

4. Listen to two people flat-hunting. What did you understand? Mark the right answers.

1. Die Wohnung hat	2. Sie ist	3. Die Miete ist	4. Die Telefonnummer ist
☐ 1 Zimmer mit Bad.	☐ 35 qm groß.	☐ 600 Euro kalt.	☐ 0911 – 62524.
☐ 2 Zimmer.	☐ 46 qm groß.	☐ 850 Euro warm.	☐ 0211 – 62424.
☐ 3 Zimmer.	☐ 55 qm groß.	☐ 850 Euro kalt.	☐ 0911 – 62424.

Check your answers in the key at the back of the book and then add up your points.

Total:	1 – 11	Oh dear, it's a pity. Please do this unit again.
	12 – 18	Not so bad. But even so, it would be a good idea to go over the vocabulary and the grammar again.
	19 – 21	Excellent. There's nothing to stop you carrying on.

Viel Verkehr! – A lot of traffic!

Next morning Frau Bruckner takes a taxi from her hotel to the Europartner office. She arrives a bit late. This is your chance to learn how to tell the time.

1 *Clocks – please match.*
Please do exercise 1 as preparation. The clocks all show different times. Match the times and clocks. Indicate whether the clock is right or wrong, fast or slow.

Armbanduhr	*watch*
Taschenuhr	*pocket watch*
Digitaluhr	*digital clock/watch*
Kuckucksuhr	*cuckoo clock*
Küchenuhr	*kitchen clock*
Bahnhofsuhr	*station clock*

Die Uhr geht …	*The clock/watch is …*
… richtig.	*… right.*
… falsch.	*… wrong.*
… vor.	*… fast.*
… nach.	*… slow.*

2 Chris Bruckner takes a taxi to the Europartner offices

→ *She is in a hurry and takes a taxi. Listen to what she says to the taxi driver. Listen to the conversation at least twice.*

→ *To help you understand what's going on, you can check up on some vocabulary via the vocabulary list.*

Bitte in die Potsdamer Straße Nummer 205.	*(To) Potsdamer Straße number 205, please.*
Nummer (die), die Nummern	*number*
Heute ist viel Verkehr.	*There is a lot of traffic today.*
Verkehr (der)	*traffic*
Haben Sie es sehr eilig?	*Are you in a great hurry?*
es eilig haben – er/sie hat es eilig	*be in a hurry*
Ja, ich habe einen Termin um 10 Uhr.	*Yes, I have an appointment at 10 o'clock.*
Termin (der), die Termine	*appointment*
um 10 Uhr	*at 10 o'clock*
Uhr (die), die Uhren/die Uhrzeit	*clock/time*
Kein Problem.	*No problem.*
Problem (das), die Probleme	*problem*
Wie weit ist es?	*How far is it?*
Wie lange brauchen wir?	*How long do we need/does it take?*
brauchen – er/sie braucht, hat gebraucht	*need*
Ungefähr vierzig Minuten.	*About forty minutes.*
ungefähr	*about*
Wir nehmen die Stadtautobahn.	*We'll take the (urban) motorway/freeway.*
Stadtautobahn (die), die Stadtautobahnen	*urban motorway/freeway*
Berlin hat viel Wasser.	*Berlin has a lot of water.*
Wasser (das)	*water*
Man sieht viele Häfen und Kanäle.	*You see a lot of docks and canals.*

sehen – du siehst, er/sie sieht, hat gesehen	*see*
Hafen (der), die Häfen	*docks, harbour, port*
Kanal (der), die Kanäle	*canal*
Wie in Venedig.	*Like in Venice.*
fast	*almost*
Ich komme leider eine Viertelstunde später.	*I'm afraid I'm going to be a quarter of an hour late. [literally: … come … later.]*
Viertelstunde (die)	*quarter of an hour*
Bis gleich.	*See you soon/later.*
Morgens ist immer Stau.	*In the mornings there's always a tailback.*
morgens	*in the morning(s)*
Stau (der), die Staus	*tailback, traffic jam*
mittags	*at lunchtime*
abends	*in the evening(s)*
Schrecklich!	*Awful! Terrible!*
Da sind wir.	*Here we are.*
Und bitte eine Quittung.	*And a receipt please.*
Quittung (die), die Quittungen	*receipt*

 The word *Stadtautobahn* is made up of *die Stadt* and *die Autobahn*. There are a lot of compound nouns in German.

 morgen**s** um acht = **immer** morgens um acht
heute Morgen = **nur** heute Morgen

3 *Who said it? Frau Bruckner or the taxi driver?*

4 *Please complete.*
Some of the nouns have disappeared from the text. Choose the right noun and complete the dialogue.

5 *What's the time?*

 6 *Speaking exercise.*
Now you're in a hurry and take a taxi. First you'll hear the example. Then you speak, using the prompt words. We'll correct you.

 7 *I'd like to …*
If you want to go to a specific place, you say nach.
Look at the photos. You want to go there. Write down the sentence you would say.
Then practise orally. First listen to the example. Then give the answers yourself.

The plural – Der Plural

In German there are 9 different ways of forming the plural. Here is an overview. Look closely at the various plural forms, and learn the plural with each noun. Careful: There are of course some nouns that don't have a plural, such as *das Wetter* or *der Verkehr* or *der Norden, der Süden.*

Singular		Plural
das Zimmer		die Zimmer
der Tag	⊕ -e	die Tage
die Stadt	umlaut ⊕ -e	die Städte
der Hafen	umlaut	die Häfen
das Kind	⊕ -er	die Kinder
das Land	umlaut ⊕ -er	die Länder
das Auto	⊕ -s	die Autos
die Frage	⊕ -n	die Fragen
die Bahn	⊕ -en	die Bahnen

The definite article is always *die* in the plural.

Always remember two things about each noun: the article in the singular, and the plural form, so: *das Auto, die Autos.*

8 *Listen to a series of nouns. Tick on whether you hear the singular or the plural form.* | 2|10

	1.	2.	3.	4.	5.	6.	7.	8.
Singular	☐	☐	☐	☐	☐	☐	☐	☐
Plural	☐	☐	☐	☐	☐	☐	☐	☐

9 *Fill in the singular or plural.*

Singular	Plural
	die Hobbys
die Adresse	
	die Kinder
das Hotel	
	die Namen
der Tag	
das Auto	
die Nummer	
	die Stunden
	die Länder
die Frage	

Telling the time (informally and officially) – Die Uhrzeit (informell und offiziell)

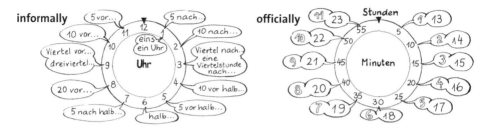

10 *Imagine you hear the exact time on the radio. "Translate" them into the form normally used in speech. Complete the sentence.*

Example: Es ist jetzt neunzehn Uhr.   → Es ist sieben.

Es ist jetzt elf Uhr dreißig.   Es ist _____ _____.

Es ist jetzt sechzehn Uhr fünfzehn.   Es ist _____ nach _____.

Es ist jetzt zehn Uhr fünfundvierzig.   Es ist _____ vor _____.

Es ist jetzt dreizehn Uhr.   Es ist _____.

Es ist jetzt neun Uhr zehn.   Es ist _____ nach _____.

Es ist jetzt neun Uhr vierzig.   Es ist _____ vor _____.

11 *Revision*

Asking the time

Wie spät ist es?	*What time is it?*
Es ist ... (3 Uhr).	*It's ... (3 o'clock).*
Ungefähr ... 3	*About ... 3.*
... (5) Minuten vor / nach ... 3.	*... (5) minutes to/past ... 3.*
Viertel vor / nach ... (4).	*(a) quarter to/past (4).*
halb drei, halb vier	*half past <u>two</u>, half past <u>three</u>*
	(halb refers forward to the next full hour.)

In the taxi

Sind Sie frei? Zum Flughafen bitte.	*Are you free? To the airport, please.*
Bitte in die ...	*To ...*
(Potsdamer Straße Nummer 205).	*(Potsdamer Straße number 205), please.*
Bitte nach ... (Tegel / Siemensstadt).	*To ... (Tegel/Siemensstadt), please.*
Ich habe es eilig / sehr eilig.	*I'm in a hurry/great hurry.*
Ich habe einen Termin um ... (10 Uhr).	*I have an appointment at ... (10 o'clock).*
Wie lange brauchen wir?	*How long do we need/does it take?*
Bitte eine Quittung.	*A receipt, please.*

Short and long vowels – Die kurzen und die langen Vokale

12 *Listen and repeat.*
Now you're going to hear some words that have either a long or a short vowel. Mark with a cross what you hear, and repeat the word.

	viel	links	abends	fast	Problem	Kanal	schrecklich	morgens
lang	☐	☐	☐	☐	☐	☐	☐	☐
kurz	☐	☐	☐	☐	☐	☐	☐	☐

13 *Listen and repeat.*

Zum Flughafen bitte.   Wie spät ist es?
Bitte nach Siemensstadt.   Viertel vor drei
Bitte eine Quittung.   Ungefähr drei.

14 *Listen and repeat.*
Now we're going to practise vowels. Try to imitate the speaker's pronunciation as accurately as you can.

eilig   Ich habe es eilig.
weit   Wie weit ist es?
ungefähr   Ungefähr vierzig Minuten.
später   Ich komme später.
heute Abend   Haben Sie heute Abend Zeit?

Cultural info (Textbook page 44)

This page is of special interest to those of you who don't live in Europe. It's easy to misjudge distances. For everybody else it's a good exercise.
It shows you how to make comparisons:
… weiter als …: Oslo ist von Frankfurt weiter als Warschau. (… further away than …: Oslo is further from Frankfurt than Warsaw.)

How far is that from Frankfurt?
6 countries – 6 capitals
Note down the capital cities.
Please complete.

Vocabulary

1. Fill in the missing word.

1. Hallo, _____ Sie frei?

2. Wohin _____ Sie?

3. _____ Siemensstadt.

4. Wie _____ brauchen wir?

5. Nicht lange. Eine halbe _____ .

6. Wir sind da. – Bitte eine _____ .

2. Mark the correct translation

1. Die Uhr geht falsch.
□ The clock is fast.
□ The watch is slow.
□ The clock is wrong.

2. Die Uhr geht vor.
□ The watch is right.
□ The clock is fast.
□ The clock is wrong.

3. Die Uhr geht nach.
□ The watch is fast.
□ The clock is slow.
□ The clock is right.

4. Ungefähr 20 Minuten.
□ About 20 minutes.
□ After 20 minutes.
□ 20 minutes past.

5. Viertel nach drei
□ Quarter to three.
□ Quarter past three.
□ 14 minutes past three.

6. Viertel vor sieben
□ 7.40.
□ 14 minutes to seven.
□ Quarter to seven.

Grammar

3. Write the official time.

1. 10 nach 3 (nachmittags) Es ist _____ _____ .

2. 5 Minuten vor 5 (nachmittags) Es ist _____ .

3. Viertel nach sechs (abends) Es ist _____ .

4. Viertel vor 8 abends Es ist _____ .

5. 7 nach halb 10 (vormittags) Es ist _____ .

6. 5 vor 12 (mittags) Es ist _____ .

4. Write the plural.

1. die Stadt _____
2. das Taxi _____
3. die Quittung _____
4. der Termin _____
5. das Büro _____
6. die Anzeige _____
7. das Haus _____
8. die Nummer _____

Check your answers in the key at the back of the book and then add up your points.

Total:
1 – 13 Before you carry on, you should really do this unit again.
14 – 22 Quite good, but not perfect yet. Please go over the dialogue and the grammar again. It'll be worth it.
23 – 26 Very good. You can carry straight on.

Die Firmenbesichtigung, Teil 1 –
Guided tour of the company, Part 1

Before lunch there is a guided tour of the company building.
You'll learn how to extend an invitation, and have a look at how a company is structured.

1 *Mark with a cross.*
Please do exercise 1 as preparation. You have your preferences when choosing a means of transport, don't you?
Maybe you'd like to explain why you prefer a particular means of transport. That's why we've suggested some phrases for giving reasons.
People use der Zug *when talking about journeys between cities,* die Bahn *more when talking about transport within a town or city.*

teuer – billig	*expensive – cheap*
schnell – langsam	*quick – slow*

2 **An invitation to dinner and a guided tour**

11A

→ *Listen to what Frau Bruckner gets to see. First though, Herr Kühne has a special sugges-*
   tion. Listen to the text at least twice.
→ *To help you understand what's going on, you can check up on some vocabulary via the*
   vocabulary list.

Es ist 11 Uhr.	*It's 11 o'clock.*
Mein Vorschlag …	*My suggestion …*
Vorschlag (der), die Vorschläge	*suggestion*
Wir machen jetzt eine Firmenbesichtigung.	*We'll do a tour of the company now.*
Firmenbesichtigung (die) (die Firma + die Besichtigung)	*(guided) tour of a company*
Und um zwölf gehen wir in die Kantine.	*And at twelve we'll go to the canteen.*
Eine Frage, …	*Can I ask you something?*
	[literally: A question, …]
Haben Sie heute Abend Zeit?	*Are you free/Do you have time this evening?*
Wir möchten Sie zum Essen einladen.	*We'd like to invite you to dinner.*
Essen (das)	*meal, dinner*
einladen – du lädst ein, er/sie lädt ein, hat eingeladen	*invite*
Ist sieben Uhr in Ordnung?	*Is seven o'clock OK?*
in Ordnung	*OK*
Ordnung (die)	*order*
Geht auch halb acht?	*Is half past seven OK, too?*

Wann fliegen Sie zurück?	*When do you fly back?*
zurückfliegen	*fly back*
– er/sie fliegt zurück, ist zurückgeflogen	
Das heißt, ich fahre mit dem Zug.	*Actually I'm going by train.*
das heißt	*actually, in fact*
mit dem Zug	*by train*
Zug (der), die Züge	*train*
Das sind nur 6 einhalb Stunden.	*It's only six and a half hours.*

11B

So, hier ist also der Vertrieb.	*Right, this is the sales department.*
Die Geschäftsleitung und das Sekretariat sind hier geradeaus.	*The management and secretary's office is straight ahead.*
Geschäftsleitung (die)	*management*
Sekretariat (das)	*secretary's office*
geradeaus	*straight ahead/on*
Wir nehmen jetzt den Aufzug.	*We'll take the lift now.*
Aufzug (der), die Aufzüge	*lift*
Keller (der), die Keller	*cellar, basement*
Einen Moment …	*Just a moment …*
Archiv (das), die Archive	*filing room, archive*

Here's a tip for learning vocabulary. Learn 5 to 10 words, then another 5 to 10 the next time. Mark the words that are important to you.

3 *Complete the text. The time expressions are missing.*
All the expressions of time have disappeared. Read the text and complete it with the right expressions.

4 *What's right? Mark with a cross.*
You remember what they said, don't you? We're going to ask you some questions.

5 *Answer with* Nein.

6 *What doesn't fit?*
These verbs take the accusative. Underline the accusative form in each case that doesn't fit.

7 *Practise the dialogue as in the example. Then listen.*

8 *Chris Bruckner's notes*

The accusative – Der Akkusativ

		masculine	feminine	neuter
personal pronoun		er	sie	es
definite article	*nom.*	der Balkon	die Wohnung	das Bad
indefinite article		ein Balkon	eine Wohnung	ein Bad
negative article		**kein** Balkon	**keine** Wohnung	**kein** Bad
definite article	*acc.*	d**en** Balkon	die Wohnung	das Bad
indefinite article		ein**en** Balkon	eine Wohnung	ein Bad
negative article		k**ein**en Balkon	**keine** Wohnung	**kein** Bad

Nominative and accusative

sein is followed by the nominative: *Das ist eine Dachwohnung. Die Wohnung ist schön.*
Most verbs are followed by the accusative: *Wir möchten einen Balkon.*
Only the masculine accusative singular has a different form from the nominative:
Ich möchte keinen Tee.

Definite and indefinite article

• When you first mention something, you use the indefinite article:
  *Das ist **eine** Dachwohnung.*
• Then you use the definite article because the thing is now known:
  ***Die** Wohnung finde ich schön.*

Negative article

• *kein-* is the negative of *ein-* and means 'no' or 'not any':
  *Wir haben **keinen** Balkon.*
• *ein-* and *kein-* are always placed in front of a noun.

9 *Fill in* den, die, das *and* der, die, das.

Nehmen Sie _____ Bus?   – Nein, _____ Bus ist schon weg.

Nehmen Sie _____ Bahn?   – Nein, _____ Bahn ist schon weg.

Nehmen Sie _____ Zug?   – Nein, _____ Zug ist schon weg.

Nehmen Sie _____ Flugzeug?   – Nein, _____ Flugzeug ist schon weg.

Nehmen Sie _____ Auto?   – Nein, _____ Auto ist kaputt.

10 *Fill in the article.*

Wir haben _____ Kantine.   – Aber _____ Kantine ist nicht gut.

Gibt es hier _____ Aufzug?   – Ja, _____ Aufzug ist da geradeaus.

Machen wir _____ Pause?   – Ja, _____ Pause ist um zwölf.

Haben Sie schon _____ Hotel?   – Ja, _____ Hotel liegt direkt im Zentrum.

Wir haben _____ Dachwohnung.   – _____ Wohnung ist sehr gemütlich.

11 *Fill in the missing part of the sentence in the accusative.*

Wir haben _____ _____ (ein Termin).

Wir nehmen _____ _____ und _____ _____. (der Bus, die Bahn)

Möchten Sie _____ _____? (ein Kaffee)

Kennen Sie _____ _____? (der Hafen)

Wir möchten _____ _____ (der Reichstag) besichtigen.

Wir möchten _____ _____ (ein Ausflug) machen.

12 *Fill in* kein- *and* ein-.

Ist das Tee? – Nein, das ist _____ Tee, das ist Kaffee.

Ist das eine Pension? – Nein, das ist _____ Pension, das ist _____ Hotel.

Ist das eine Telefonnummer? – Nein, das ist _____ Telefonnummer, das ist _____ Passwort.

Ist das ein Vorname? – Nein, das ist _____ Vorname, das ist _____ Nachname.

Ist Australien ein Land? – Nein, Australien ist _____ Land, es ist _____ Erdteil.

Ist das eine Vorwahlnummer? – Nein, das ist _____ Vorwahlnummer, das ist _____ Postleitzahl.

13 kein- *+ noun or* nicht *+ verb – Please negate.*

Ich habe ein Auto. Ich habe _____ Auto.

Ich fliege. Ich fliege _____.

Ich fliege gern. Ich fliege _____ _____.

Ich fahre mit dem Auto. Ich fahre _____ mit dem Auto.

Ich habe Zeit. Ich habe _____ Zeit.

Ich komme. Ich komme _____.

Ich habe eine Frage. Ich habe _____ Frage.

14 *Revision*

Inviting someone

Haben Sie … (heute Abend / morgen / …) Zeit?	*Are you free/Do you have time … (this evening/tomorrow/…)?*
Wir möchten Sie zum Essen einladen.	*We'd like to invite you to dinner.*
Gerne. Vielen Dank.	*Fine./I'd like that. Thank you very much.*
Ist … (sieben Uhr) in Ordnung?	*Is … (seven o'clock) OK?*
– Ja natürlich. / Geht auch halb acht?	*– Yes, of course./Would half past seven be OK too?/Is half past seven OK too?*

Stress

15 *Mark with a cross, and repeat.*
A very large number of words in German are stressed on the first syllable, as in English. Listen closely. Mark with a cross which syllable is stressed. Then repeat the word.

1ˢᵗ 2ⁿᵈ **syllable**	1ˢᵗ 2ⁿᵈ **syllable**	1ˢᵗ 2ⁿᵈ **syllable**	1ˢᵗ 2ⁿᵈ **syllable**
☐ ☐ Straße	☐ ☐ morgens	☐ ☐ Geschäft	☐ ☐ München
☐ ☐ Verkehr	☐ ☐ Reise	☐ ☐ Besuch	☐ ☐ Norden
☐ ☐ Quittung	☐ ☐ machen	☐ ☐ Zimmer	☐ ☐ gestern
☐ ☐ Nummer	☐ ☐ Beruf	☐ ☐ Mittag	☐ ☐ Frage
☐ ☐ Termin	☐ ☐ Handy	☐ ☐ Berlin	☐ ☐ Vorschlag

16 *Mark with a cross, and repeat.*
Now here are some three-syllable words. First listen, then mark with a cross which syllable of the word is stressed. At the end, repeat the words.

1ˢᵗ 2ⁿᵈ 3ʳᵈ **syllable**	1ˢᵗ 2ⁿᵈ 3ʳᵈ **syllable**
☐ ☐ ☐ Stadtrundfahrt	☐ ☐ ☐ Fahrkarte
☐ ☐ ☐ Anzeige	☐ ☐ ☐ sympathisch
☐ ☐ ☐ Telefon	☐ ☐ ☐ Kantine
☐ ☐ ☐ arbeiten	☐ ☐ ☐ Geburtsort
☐ ☐ ☐ Adresse	☐ ☐ ☐ Grammatik

17 *An exercise for experts. Mark with a cross.*
Don't worry if the stress is new for you. The more you hear and speak German texts, the more you'll get into the swing of it.
Listen and mark the stressed syllable with a cross.

1ˢᵗ 2ⁿᵈ 3ʳᵈ 4ᵗʰ **syllable**	1ˢᵗ 2ⁿᵈ 3ʳᵈ 4ᵗʰ **syllable**
☐ ☐ ☐ ☐ buchstabieren	☐ ☐ ☐ ☐ besichtigen
☐ ☐ ☐ ☐ interessant	☐ ☐ ☐ ☐ geradeaus
☐ ☐ ☐ ☐ Informatik	☐ ☐ ☐ ☐ Entschuldigung
☐ ☐ ☐ ☐ Information	

Cultural info (Textbook page 48)

There's a surprise waiting for you. Start at START. Find the way through to the end.
The letters make up two sentences. What are the sentences?
Have fun!

Weg (der)   *way*
Ziel (das)   *destination, goal*

Vocabulary

1. *Mark the correct translation with a cross.*

1. die Einladung
☐ guided tour
☐ invitation
☐ suggestion

2. mit dem Zug
☐ by plane
☐ on the motorway
☐ by train

3. Das macht Spaß.
☐ It's terrible.
☐ It's fun.
☐ There's no room here.

4. zum Essen einladen
☐ have an appointment
☐ be late
☐ invite someone to dinner

5. heute Abend
☐ this evening
☐ later today
☐ in the evening

6. der Vorschlag
☐ water
☐ meal
☐ suggestion

2. *Fill in the right verb.*

1. Zeit _____

2. zum Essen _____

3. ein Taxi _____

4. mit dem Zug _____

5. zu Fuß _____

6. einen Termin _____

Grammar

3. ein- *or* kein-? *– Please complete*

1. Gibt es hier _____ Telefon?   – Nein, hier gibt es _____ Telefon.

2. Gibt es hier _____ Aufzug?   – Nein, hier gibt es _____ Aufzug.

3. Gibt es hier _____ Kantine?   – Nein, hier gibt es _____ Kantine.

4. Gibt es hier _____ Vertrieb?   – Nein, hier gibt es _____ Vertrieb.

5. Gibt er hier _____ Firmen-   – Nein, hier gibt es _____ Firmenbesichtigung?   besichtigung.

6. Gibt es hier _____ Chef?   – Nein, hier gibt es _____ Chef.

4. *The accusative is missing. Please complete.*

1. der Hafen   – Wir besichtigen heute _____ _____ .

2. der Bus   – Wir nehmen _____ _____ .

3. der Stau   – Siehst du _____ _____ ?

4. der Zug   – Wir nehmen _____ _____ um achtzehn Uhr.

5. der Aufzug   – Nehmen Sie _____ _____ ?

6. die Kantine   – Gehen wir in _____ _____ ?

7. der Raum   – Wir haben _____ _____ Nummer 3.

8. die Arbeit   – Wer macht _____ _____ ?

Check your answers in the key at the back of the book and then add up your points.

Total:	1 – 13	It would be a good idea to do this unit again straightaway.
	14 – 22	Pretty good. But it wouldn't hurt to go over the dialogues and the grammar again.
	23 – 26	Excellent. If you like, you could go over the vocabulary again, otherwise you can carry straight on.

Die Firmenbesichtigung, Teil 2 –
Guided tour of the company, Part 2

1 *What do you see? Please match.*
The names of various departments are mentioned on the company tour. Before you listen to
the text mark the German words that come from English. There are actually quite a few.

die Buchhaltung	*accounts (department)*
das Controlling	*controlling (department)*
die IT-Abteilung	*IT department*
die Redaktion, die Redaktionen	*editorial department*
die Herstellung/Produktion	*production (department)*
die Marketing-Abteilung	*marketing department*
der Vertrieb	*sales (department)*
der Versand	*despatch department*
das Lager	*warehouse, stock-room*

2 Left, right, straight on

12A

→ *Now follow us round the rooms and departments on the ground floor. At the end we'll*
meet up in the canteen. First listen to the dialogue.

→ *To help you understand what's going on, you can check up on some vocabulary via the*
vocabulary list.

Wir sind jetzt im Erdgeschoss.	*We're now on the ground floor.*
Erdgeschoss (das)	*ground floor*
Hier links ist das Informationszentrum.	*Here on the left is the information centre.*
links – rechts – geradeaus	*(on the) left – (on the) right – straight on*
Informationszentrum (das), die Informations-zentren (die Information + das Zentrum)	*information centre*
Konferenzraum (der), die Konferenzräume (die Konferenz + der Raum)	*conference room*
Da macht die Arbeit Spaß.	*Work is fun there.*
Den Empfang und die Redaktionen haben Sie schon gesehen.	*You've already seen reception and the editorial departments.*
gegenüber	*opposite*
Ich verstehe.	*I see/understand.*
verstehen – er/sie versteht, hat verstanden	*understand*
besichtigen – er/sie besichtigt, hat besichtigt	*look round, see*
Das ist eine Viertelstunde zu Fuß.	*It's a quarter of an hour's walk/quarter of an hour on foot.*
glauben – er/sie glaubt, hat geglaubt	*believe, think*
Raum (der), die Räume	*room*

12B

At the entrance to the canteen there is a sign. Read what it says. If you don't understand everything, you can look up the words here.

Selbstbedienung (die)	*self-service*
Geöffnet von … bis	*Open from … to*
Gäste-Casino (das)	*visitors' canteen*
Gast (der), die Gäste	*visitor, guest*
Anmeldung (die)	*booking, reception*
Kantinenleitung (die) (die Kantine + die Leitung)	*canteen management*

Now listen to the text. Then read it out loud yourself.

3 *What's the right order?*
Listen again to the order in which the departments are visited. Note down the order of the departments from B to F. We've already done the information centre (A) for you.

4 *This is Europartner. Read the text and draw the route on the sketch.*
If you take the right route, you'll soon get there and be able to sit down and enjoy your lunch.

5 *Frau Bruckner tells Herr Kühne what she's seen. Write the correct form.*

6 *Please match.*
The opening times of shops and public buildings in Germany are fixed by law, and regulations are only gradually becoming more flexible. Opening times give you a pretty good idea of where you are at a particular time. Read the signs and match the drawings to them. If you don't understand all the words, here is the vocabulary:

Montag	*Monday*	Freitag	*Friday*
Dienstag	*Tuesday*	Sonnabend / Samstag	*Saturday*
Mittwoch	*Wednesday*	Sonntag	*Sunday*
Donnerstag	*Thursday*		

Sprechstunde (die)	*Surgery*
geöffnet / geschlossen (von … bis …)	*open / closed (from … to …)*
(Montag) geschlossen … bis …	*closed (on Monday) … till …*

7 *Speaking exercise. What would you like to see? First listen to the example, then answer.*

8 *Please write.*
Some important information is missing in this calendar. Write in the days of the week.

Word order I – Satzstellung I

I	II		I	II		
Wir	**arbeiten**	bis 11.	Dann	**machen**	wir	Pause.
Wir	**machen**	Pause.	Um zwölf	**gehen**	wir	in die Kantine.
Wir	**gehen**	in die Kantine.	Geradeaus	**ist**		die Kantine.

- In German, sentences often begin with a word or expression giving information about the time or place. Often, too, there is a link back to the preceding sentence (for example *Dann* …). The verb is nevertheless always in position 2. The noun or pronoun come after it.
- Statements and questions starting with a question word: The verb is always in position II. Questions without a question word: The verb is in position I.
Wann **gehen** *wir in die Kantine?*
Gehen *wir in die Kantine?*

9 *What's the sentence?*
This is all about word order. We ask you a question. You have part of the reply. Write the answer.

- Was machen wir um 10 Uhr? ▶ | Wir | | bis 11 Uhr | | arbeiten |

_____

- Und dann? ▶ | eine Pause | | wir | | Dann | | machen |

_____

- Und was machen wir dann? ▶ | machen | | Um 11 Uhr 15 | | wir | | eine Firmenbesichtigung |

_____

- Wie lange machen wir die Firmenbesichtigung? ▶ | die Firmenbesichtigung | | bis 12 | | dauert |

_____

- Was machen wir um 12? ▶ | in die Kantine | | wir | | Um 12 | | gehen |

_____

- Wie lange essen wir? ▶ | Wir | | essen | | bis eins |

_____

- Und dann? ▶ | wir | | Dann | | arbeiten | | bis 3 |

_____

- Was machen wir um 3? ▶ | machen | | Um 3 | | wir | | eine Stadtrundfahrt |

_____

- Wann sind wir zurück? ▶ | im Hotel | | zurück | | wir | | sind | | Um 7 |

_____

10 *What's the sentence?*

jetzt	Wir machen eine Firmenbesichtigung.	Jetzt machen _____
um 12 Uhr	Ich komme in die Kantine.	_____
heute Abend	Ich habe Zeit.	_____
morgen	Ich fahre zurück nach München.	_____
vielleicht	Ich nehme den Zug.	_____
dann	Ich rufe an.	_____

11 *Das* Krankenzimmer - *The sickbay*
First read the dialogue. Then listen to the words.

der Kopf	*head*
das Haar	*hair*
das Auge, die Augen	*eye*
der Mund	*mouth*
der Zahn, die Zähne	*tooth*
der Hals	*neck*
die Hand, die Hände	*hand*
der Arm, die Arme	*arm*
der Bauch	*stomach*
das Bein, die Beine	*leg*

Frau Bruckner:	Was haben Sie hier?
Herr Heinrich:	Das ist das Krankenzimmer. Deshalb das Plakat.
Frau Bruckner:	Ah ja. Haben Sie einen Notarzt im Haus?
Herr Heinrich:	Nein, nein, den rufen wir.
	Tut Ihnen was weh? Ich hoffe nicht.
Frau Bruckner:	Nein, zum Glück, ich bin ganz gesund.

12 *Revision and extension*

The sickbay

krank – gesund	*ill – well, healthy*
Krankheit (die)	*illness, disease*
Gesundheit (die)	*health*
wehtun	*hurt*
Notarzt (der), die Notärzte	*emergency doctor*
Schmerzen (die Plural)	*pain, ache*
Zahnschmerzen (die Plural) (der Zahn + die Schmerzen)	*toothache*

13 *Which syllable is stressed? Listen closely and underline.*

1	2	3	4	5	6
Emp	fang				
Re	dak	tion			
Erd	ge	schoss			
ge	ra	de	aus		
ge	gen	ü	ber		
Kon	fe	renz	räu	me	
In	for	ma	tions	zen	trum
Fir	men	be	sich	ti	gung

Cultural info (Textbook page 52)
What do I do? What do I say? – Some little tips

Hello and goodbye

People usually shake hands when saying *Guten Tag or Auf Wiedersehen*. But when do you do it, and when don't you?

Handshaking is always rather formal. You greet business partners like this. Good friends or colleagues see each other daily, and they of course don't shake hands. They just say *Hallo, Guten Tag* or *Grüß Gott* (in the south), often adding the person's name, and that's it. On special occasions and when it's someone's birthday, friends and colleagues are also more formal and shake the person's hand.

„Mahlzeit"

At work you often hear people saying *Mahlzeit* (literally: "mealtime") to each other around the middle of the day. You say *Mahlzeit*, and the reply is *Mahlzeit* too. Then you go to the canteen or have something to eat in your office. People only say *Mahlzeit* at work, never at home or in a restaurant.

Help! I'm going to be late!

Punctuality is important in Germany. People who are repeatedly late for business meetings make a bad impression. But it can happen of course. Then you can phone and say: *Ich komme leider eine halbe Stunde später.* Or you can apologize with the sentence: *Tut mir leid, dass ich zu spät komme.*

75

Vocabulary

1. *What's the word?*

1. | fe | renz | kon | raum | 2. | ti | kan | ne | 3. | dung | la | ein |

4. | ger | la | 5. | trum | zen | tions | infor | ma | 6. | dak | re | tion |

2. *Write correctly.*

1. hieristkeinplatz _____   4. dasmachtspaß _____

2. ichglaubenicht _____   5. ichverstehe _____

3. dageradeaus _____

Grammar

3. *Write the sentence.*

1. Wir besichtigen den Hafen.   - Heute _____

2. Wir nehmen den Bus.   - Um eins _____

3. Wir haben Raum 3.   - Morgen _____

4. Das Casino ist geöffnet.   - Bis 18 Uhr _____

5. Wir besichtigen die Firma.   - Am Vormittag _____

6. Ich fahre wieder zurück.   - Mittwoch _____

4. *Note down the verbs with special forms in the singular.*

	sehen	du siehst	er / sie sieht
1.	_____	_____	_____
2.	_____	_____	_____
3.	_____	_____	_____
4.	_____	_____	_____
5.	_____	_____	_____

glauben	fahren
verstehen	nehmen
mögen	schlafen
besichtigen	wohnen
geben	möchten
fliegen	

Listening Comprehension

(2|26)

5. *First listen to the dialogue between a taxi driver and a tourist. Then answer the questions.*

1. Wo ist der Tourist?   In _ _ _ _ _ _ .

2. Wie viel kostet die Fahrt?   Circa _ _ _ _ _ _ _ Euro.

3. Wohin möchte er?   Ins _ _ _ _ _ _ _ .

4. Wie fährt er?   Mit der _ _ _ _ _ _ .

5. Hat er einen Stadtplan?   _ _ , natürlich.

Check your answers in the key at the back of the book and then add up your points.

Total:	1 - 14 Oh dear, that's a pity. Please do this unit again.
	15 – 23 Not so bad. But even so, it would be a good idea to go over the dialogues and the grammar again.
	24 – 27 Excellent. There's nothing to stop you carrying on.

Das Frühstück – Breakfast

In this lesson you're going to learn something about a typical part of German life: breakfast. Claudia talks about her family over breakfast. As she does so, the possessive articles *mein* and *dein* are used.

1 *Please match.*
Listen to how the items on the breakfast table are pronounced, and repeat out loud.

Brötchen (das),	roll		Marmelade (die)	jam
die Brötchen			Messer (das), die Messer	knife
Butter (die)	butter		Löffel (der), die Löffel	spoon
Brot (das), die Brote	(slice of) bread		Gabel (die), die Gabeln	fork
Ei (das), die Eier	egg		Käse (der)	cheese
Teller (der), die Teller	plate		Obst (das)	fruit
Tasse (die), die Tassen	cup		Serviette (die), die Servietten	napkin

2 Breakfast is ready
It's all right for Robert. He doesn't have to go to work or to the university. He gets up late and goes into the kitchen. Claudia has laid the breakfast table there.
Now listen to how Claudia greets Robert and what there is for breakfast. Listen to the text at least twice. And here's some help with the vocabulary again.

Hast du gut geschlafen?	Did you sleep well?
schlafen – du schläfst, er / sie schläft, hat geschlafen	sleep
Niki ist schon weg.	Niki has already left.
weg sein – er / sie ist weg	be gone
Es gibt gleich Frühstück.	Breakfast won't be a minute.
gleich	in a minute, straightaway
Keinen Tee. (= Ich möchte keinen Tee.)	No tea. (= I don't want tea.)
Ich mag lieber Kaffee.	I prefer coffee.
mögen – er / sie mag, hat gemocht	like
lieber mögen	prefer
Und dann ein Brötchen mit Butter und Marmelade.	And then a roll with butter and jam.
Eier sind auch da.	There are some eggs, too.
Sag mal, Claudia, deine Eltern, wo wohnen die eigentlich?	Tell me, Claudia, your parents, where do they live actually?
Eltern (die Plural)	parents
eigentlich	actually, in fact, really
Ganz in der Nähe.	Very nearby.
Übrigens, meine Schwester ist da.	By the way, my sister is here.

mein, meine	*my*
Schwester (die), die Schwestern	*sister*
Sie ist gestern aus Sydney gekommen.	*She came from Sydney yesterday.*
gestern	*yesterday*
Sie hat dort ein paar Monate gearbeitet.	*She's been working there for a few months.*
Regisseurin (die) – Regisseur (der)	*director, producer*
Mein Bruder Ralf geht noch zur Schule.	*My brother Ralf is still in school.*
Bruder (der), die Brüder	*brother*
zur Schule gehen	*go to school, be in school*
Schule (die), die Schulen	*school*
Er wohnt natürlich zu Hause.	*He lives at home of course.*
Wir besuchen heute meine Eltern.	*We'll visit my parents today.*
besuchen – er/sie besucht, hat besucht	*visit*
Was meinst du?	*What do you think?*
meinen – er/sie meint, hat gemeint	*think*
dann lerne ich endlich deine Geschwister kennen	*then I'll get to know your brothers and sisters at last*
kennen lernen – er/sie lernt kennen, hat kennen gelernt	*get to know*
Geschwister (die Plural)	*brothers and sisters*

3 *Please complete.*
These questions and sentences can all be spoken at the breakfast table. Fill in the gaps.

4 *Reconstruct the text .*
Find the most suitable word. And remember: the meaning must fit, not just the form.

Unspecific quantities have no article: *Ich möchte Brot mit Butter und Marmelade.*
The article is used with a specific quantity and in the negative: *Ich möchte ein Brötchen, kein Brot.*

5 *Please complete.*
This is all about the modal verb mögen, möchten *is used in polite questions and answers.*

6 *Please complete. Here you practise* mein *and* dein *in the nominative.*

7 *Speaking exercise*
Now you can decide what you would like. Listen to the question. Then read the prompts and reply. The picture gives you the answer.

8 *Robert's diary – Some important words are missing.*

Verbs – Verben: mögen

		mögen
Singular	ich	**mag**
	du	**magst**
	er/sie	**mag**
Plural	wir	mögen
	ihr	mögt
	sie/Sie	mögen

mögen:

There are special forms in the singular: *mag, magst, mag.*

Notice the difference between *ich mag* (I like) and *ich möchte* (I'd like):

Möchten Sie Kaffee?
Nein danke, ich möchte lieber Tee. (= Bitte einen Tee.)
Ich mag keinen Kaffee. (= Ich trinke keinen Kaffee.)

Ralf mag Katrin. Aber Katrin mag Guido.

9 *What doesn't fit? Please cross out.*

Ich mag ...

| Test | keinen Tee | Müsli | Ei | das Brot | Dachwohnung | Eltern | Christine | Wort |

| meinen Beruf | Sydney | Australien | Berlin | die Übungen | deinen Bruder | Sprache |

Article *kein*; possessive articles *mein/dein* – Artikel *kein*; Possessivartikel *mein/dein*

		masculine		feminine		neuter	
Personal pronouns	nom. sing.	**er**		**sie**		**es**	
indefinite article		ein	Bruder	eine	Schwester	ein	Haus
negative article		kein		keine		kein	
possessive article		mein		meine		mein	
		dein		deine		dein	
indefinite article	acc. sing.	einen	Bruder	eine	Schwester	ein	Haus
negative article		keinen	Bruder	keine	Schwester	kein	Haus
possessive article		meinen	Bruder	meine	Schwester	mein	Haus
		deinen		deine		dein	

The possessive articles *mein-* and *dein-* have the same endings as *kein-*.

10 *Please complete.*
You can make something negative with nicht *and* kein. kein- *is always placed before a noun.*

Haben Sie ein Auto?   – Nein, ich habe _____ Auto.

Haben Sie eine Uhr?   – Nein, ich habe _____ Uhr.

Haben Sie Geschwister?   – Nein, ich habe _____ Geschwister.

Haben Sic Zeit?   – Nein, ich habe _____ Zeit.

Haben Sie Semesterferien? – Nein, ich habe _____ Semesterferien.

Haben Sie Hunger?   – Nein, ich habe _____ Hunger.

11 mein *and* dein. *Fill in.*

Markus, ist das _____ Fahrkarte?

Nina, ist das _____ Handy?

Klaus, ist das _____ Kaffee?

Ralf, ist das _____ Frühstück?

Das ist _____ Bruder. – Kennst du _____ Bruder?

Das ist _____ Schwester. – Kennst du _____ Schwester?

12 *Please complete.*
Somebody here is not very friendly. He says very clearly what is his. Careful when you get to the last sentence.

Das ist nicht _____ Frühstück, das ist _____ Frühstück.

Das ist nicht _____ Schwester, das ist _____ Schwester.

Das ist nicht _____ Fahrkarte, das ist _____ Fahrkarte.

Das ist nicht _____ Auto, das ist _____ Auto.

Das ist nicht _____ Uhr, das ist _____ Uhr.

Das ist nicht _____ Problem, das ist _____ Problem.

13 *Put the sentences in the right order and write the text.*

Niki heißt Bat mit Familiennamen.

Aber er möchte die Sprache gern lernen.

Die Eltern sind 1960 nach Deutschland gekommen. Jetzt haben sie ein chinesisches Restaurant.

Das ist das Restaurant in der Hafenstraße. Das Essen dort ist sehr gut, sagt man.

Er wohnt und arbeitet in Berlin und ist auch hier geboren.

Deshalb ist nur der Familienname Chinesisch, nicht der Vorname. Er spricht auch kein Chinesisch.

14 *Revision*

Likes and dislikes

(Kaffee/…) mag ich nicht.	I don't like … (coffee/…).
Ich mag keine/-n … (Milch/Kaffee …).	I don't like (any) … (milk/coffee …).
Ich trinke … (keinen Kaffee).	I don't drink … (coffee/…).
Ich mag lieber … (Tee/…).	I prefer … (tea/…).
Ich esse … (keinen Salat).	I don't eat … (any) (salad).
Ich mag … (Birgit/…) sehr.	I like … (Birgit/…) a lot.
Ich mag … (Lisa/…) nicht so sehr.	I don't like … (Lisa/…) much.
Ich finde … (Claudia/Robert/Frau Klein)	I (don't) think/(don't) find …
sympathisch/nicht so sympathisch.	(Claudia/Robert/Frau Klein) (is) (so) nice.

a and ä

ä is the umlaut belonging to the vowel *a*. Some verbs have *ä* in the *du* and *er/sie* form *(fahren - du fährst, er/sie fährt; einladen – du lädst ein, er/sie lädt ein)*; *ä* is also used in the plural of some nouns *(Vater – Väter)*.

15 *Listen and repeat. Try to imitate the speaker's pronunciation as closely as possible.*

fahren	–	Claudia fährt.	der Hafen	–	die Häfen
schlafen	–	Robert schläft schon.	der Kanal	–	die Kanäle
das Bad	–	zwei Bäder	das Land	–	die Länder
mein Vater	–	die Väter	der Vorschlag	–	die Vorschläge

u und ü

u has the umlaut *ü*. This *ü* can be short or long. We're going to practise it now.

16 *Listen and repeat.*
Try to imitate the speaker's pronunciation as closely as possible.

Mutter und Mütter	viel früher
Bruder und Brüder	übrigens
das Frühstück	er fliegt zurück
vier Brüder	eine Viertelstunde früher
viel Glück	Das ist gemütlich.

Cultural info – Jumbled words (Textbook page 56)

If there's a word you don't know, look it up in the wordlist.
Find the words. There are 7 generic terms. Note down the article too.

der Vater (= Papa), die Väter	der Cousin, die Cousins
die Mutter (= Mama), die Mütter	die Cousine, die Cousinen
der Mann, die Männer	der Onkel, die Onkel
die Frau, die Frauen	die Tante, die Tanten
das Kind, die Kinder	der Enkel, die Enkel
das Baby, die Babys	die Enkelin, die Enkelinnen
die Eltern (Plural)	der Schwiegersohn, die Schwiegersöhne
der Sohn, die Söhne	die Schwiegertochter, die Schwiegertöchter
die Tochter, die Töchter	der Schwiegervater, die Schwiegerväter
der Bruder, die Brüder	die Schwiegermutter, die Schwiegermütter
die Schwester, die Schwestern	
der Großvater (= Opa), die Großväter	
die Großmutter (= Oma), die Großmütter	

Vocabulary

1. Here are some important expressions that you'll want to use often. Match the right translation.

1. Christian ist schon weg.
☐ Christian has already arrived.
☐ Christian is here now.
☐ Christian has already left.

3. Jan geht noch zur Schule.
☐ Jan is going to school.
☐ Jan doesn't go to school.
☐ Jan is still at school.

5. Übrigens …
☐ Actually …
☐ By the way …
☐ Over …

2. Sag mal … hast du Hunger?
☐ Say again … are you hungry.
☐ Tell me … what is hunger?
☐ Tell me … are you hungry?

4. Was meinst du?
☐ What does she mean?
☐ What do you think?
☐ Was that right?

6. Wirklich?
☐ Ready?
☐ Really?
☐ Why?

2. Fill in the appropriate word.

1. Mutter und _____

2. Bruder und _____

3. Oma und _____

4. Tochter und _____

5. Onkel und _____

6. Schwiegervater und _____

7. Mann und _____

Grammar

3. There is some trouble here about what belongs to whom. Fill in the correct form. The possessive article is missing.

1. Das ist mein Handy, nicht _____ Handy.

2. Das ist mein Auto, nicht _____ Auto.

3. Das ist mein Problem, nicht _____ Problem.

4. Das ist mein Lieblingsessen, nicht _____ Lieblingsessen.

5. Das ist meine Wohnung, nicht _____ Wohnung.

6. Das sind meine Geschwister, nicht _____ Geschwister.

4. Fill in mögen *or* möchten.

1. _____ du Brot oder Brötchen?

2. Ich _____ lieber Brötchen.

3. Ich _____ keinen Tee.

4. _____ du Kaffee? – Ja, gern.

5. _____ du deine Schwester Kerstin?

6. Ich _____ Kerstin sehr.

Check your answers in the key at the back of the book and then add up your points.

Total:
1 – 13	Before you carry on, you really should do this unit again.
14 – 21	Quite good, but not perfect yet. Please go over the dialogue and the grammar again.
22 – 25	Very good. You can carry straight on.

Wir besuchen meine Familie – We're visiting my family

This lesson is all about the family. People meet and talk. You'll learn the names of countries and languages. The past forms of *sein* and *haben* open up new ways for you to express yourself.

1 *Listen to what Claudia has to say.*
Claudia and Robert set off straight after breakfast and visit her parents during the morning. Robert is looking forward to meeting Claudia's brother and sister.
On the way to her parents, Claudia talks about her family. Listen to what she says and write the names on the sketch.

2 The family
→ *Now listen to the family greeting each other and hear what they have to say. Listen to the conversation at least twice.*

Mama is the familiar form of *Mutter. Papa* the familiar form of *Vater.*

→ *If you want to have a closer look at the words and sentences, here they are:*

Wir besuchen meine Familie	*We're visiting my family.*
lange nicht gesehen = Ich habe dich lange nicht gesehen.	*long time no see = I haven't seen you for a long time.*
Du bist sicher Robert.	*You must be Robert.*
sicher	*certain(ly)*
Claudia hat schon viel von dir erzählt.	*Claudia has told us a lot about you.*
Wirklich?	*Really?*
Mama = Mutter (die), die Mütter	*mum(my) = mother*
Papa = Vater (der), die Väter	*dad(dy) = father*
Wie gefällt Ihnen Berlin?	*How do you like Berlin?*
gefallen – er / sie / es gefällt, hat gefallen	*like*
Das war in einer Sprachenschule in England.	*That was in a language school in England.*
Sprachenschule (die), die Sprachenschulen (die Sprache + die Schule)	*language school*
ich hatte Semesterferien	*I was on (university) vacation*
Semesterferien (die Plural) (das Semester + die Ferien)	*(university) vacation*
Da bin ich nach England gefahren und habe Englisch gelernt.	*I went to England and learned English.*
Englisch	*English*
lernen – er / sie lernt, hat gelernt	*learn*
Und da waren auch Claudia und Niki.	*And Claudia and Niki were there too.*
Und jetzt sprechen Sie die Sprache perfekt, nicht wahr?	*And now you speak the language perfectly, don't you?*

perfekt	perfect(ly)
Kinder, ihr habt bestimmt Hunger.	Children, I'm sure you're hungry.
Ich habe dein Lieblingsessen gekocht.	I've cooked your favourite meal.
Lieblingsessen (das)	favourite meal
Das siehst du gleich.	You'll see in a minute.

3 *What is the correct order?*
Put the conversations in the right order. The greeting comes first of course.

4 *Please complete.*
war and hatte *occur in the dialogue. They are the past tense forms of* sein *and* haben. *Do this short gap-fill exercise.*

5 *What is right?*
Mark the right sentences with a cross.

6 *Here are all the five people in the conversation. Who said what?*
Please match.

7 *Speaking exercise.*
First read the example and the prompts. Then listen to the question and reply.

8 *Jumbled letters*
Claudia's favourite meal is hidden in this letter matrix. There are three words: a vegetable that is eaten in the spring up till June, and what is eaten with it.
And here's another tip: look at the word Legraps. This is an anagram of the main ingredient.

Find Claudia's favourite food.

Past of *sein* and *haben* / Präteritum von *sein* und *haben*: *war* und *hatte*

		sein	haben
Singular	ich	war	hatte
	du	warst	hattest
	er / sie / es	war	hatte
Plural	wir	waren	hatten
	ihr	wart	hattet
	sie / Sie	waren	hatten

Once you've learned *war* and *hatte* and some perfect forms, you can talk about things that happened in the past.

9 *Fill in the missing verbs.*
Here you can report something in the past.

Wir _____ (sein) gestern zu Hause bei Guido. Guidos Brüder _____ (sein)

auch da. Guidos Schwester _____ (haben) aber keine Zeit. Sie _____ (sein)

bei Christine. Das ist eine Freundin. Die Eltern _____ (sein) in der Stadt.

Ich _____ (haben) meine CDs mit. Es _____ (sein) sehr gemütlich.

Personal pronouns in the accusative/Personalpronomen: Akkusativ: *Ich habe dich lange nicht gesehen.*

Singular	ich	Verstehst du	**mich**	?
	du	Ich habe	**dich**	lange nicht gesehen.
	er / sie / es		**ihn / sie / es**	
Plural	wir	Verstehst du	**uns**	?
	ihr	Ich habe	**euch**	lange nicht gesehen.
	sie / Sie		**sie / Sie**	

• Most verbs take the accusative. *Ich finde **deinen Bruder** sehr sympathisch.*
• An article + noun can be replaced by a pronoun: *Ich finde **ihn** sehr sympathisch.*
  A pronoun is used when you want to avoid repeating a noun.

10 *Replace the noun with a pronoun.*

Wie finden Sie das Essen?   – Ich finde _____ gut.

Bitte rufen Sie Herrn Schneider an.   – Ich habe _____ schon angerufen. Er ist nicht da.

Wie findest du Evas Schwester?   – Ich finde _____ interessant.

Hast du die Adresse?   – Ja, ich habe _____.

Brauchen Sie den Wagen?   – Ja, ich brauche _____ heute.

Kennen Sie die Leute?   – Nein, ich kenne _____ auch nicht.

11 *Noun + noun*

The word Lieblingsessen *occurred in the text. You can also use* Lieblings- *with other words.*
Try it. You'll see from the meaning of the words which ones it can be used with.

| stadt | bruder | dienstag | schwester | brot | film |

| hotel | anmeldung | regisseur | zimmer |

Lieblings_____   Lieblings_____   Lieblings_____   Lieblings_____

Lieblings_____   Lieblings_____   Lieblings_____

12 *Countries and Nationalities*

Here's a table with names of countries and nationalities. Complete the table with the
missing words. All the adjectives end in -isch.

Land	Nationalität	Land	Nationalität
	Tschechisch		Chinesisch
Polen			Koreanisch
Russland		Österreich	
Türkei			Schweizerisch
Japan			Mexikanisch
	Spanisch	Ungarn	
	Italienisch		Griechisch

The names of languages are written with a capital letter, as in English:
Das ist Französisch.
Wie heißt das auf Französisch?

13 *Revision*

Asking someone to say something

Sag mal, … (wo wohnst du eigentlich)?	*Tell me, … (where in fact do you live)?*
Was meinst du?	*What do you think?*
Wie gefällt dir / Ihnen … (die Stadt)?	*How do you like … (the city)?*
Woher kennst du / kennen Sie …?	*How do you know …?*
Ich habe noch eine Frage.	*I have a / another question.*
Eine Frage, …	*A question, …*
Sprichst du / Sprechen Sie … (Deutsch)?	*Do you speak … (German)?*
– Ja natürlich. / Ja, aber nicht gut. / Nur wenig.	*– Yes, of course. / Yes, but not well. / Only a little.*
Sprechen Sie perfekt … (Deutsch)? –	*Do you speak perfect … (German)?*
– Nicht perfekt, aber gut.	*– Not perfect, but good.*

Endung -(i)sch

14 *Listen closely and repeat.*

Französisch	Sprechen Sie Französisch?	Chinesisch	Ist das Chinesisch?
Englisch	Sprechen Sie Englisch?	Australisch	Ist das Australisch?
Deutsch	Sprechen Sie Deutsch?	Irisch	Ist das Irisch?
Italienisch	Sprechen Sie Italienisch?	Griechisch	Ist das Griechisch?
Spanisch	Sprechen Sie Spanisch?	Polnisch	Ist das Polnisch?
Japanisch	Sprechen Sie Japanisch?	Tschechisch	Ist das Tschechisch?

15 a. *Now listen to the conversation between the two friends. The stessed syllables are underlined. Listen closely.*

Melanie:	Sag mal, hast du eigentlich Geschwister?
Lisa:	Klar.
Melanie:	Und wie viele?
Lisa:	Drei. Zwei Schwestern und einen Bruder.
Melanie:	Toll! Ich habe leider keine Geschwister.
Lisa:	Macht doch nichts. Du hast ja deine Freunde.
	Sag mal, was machst du heute Abend?
	Wir machen eine Party. Zu Hause.
Melanie:	Ja, prima, und wann?
Lisa:	Na so gegen acht.
Melanie:	Ich komme. Wo wohnst du?
Lisa:	In der Baumstr. 10.
Melanie:	Ah, da kommt mein Bus ... Also dann bis heute Abend. Tschüs.
Lisa.	Tschüs!

15 b. *Now listen and speak at the same time.*

Cultural info (Textbook page 60)

c) Bavaria is well-known for its beer. Not many people know that more beer is brewed in northern Germany than in Bavaria. Dortmund beer is famous.
f) This of course is Hamburg.

Here are six drawings. Match the six texts to the right drawings.

Vocabulary

1. Supply the language: for example England – Englisch.

1. Frankreich _____   5. Australien _____

2. Polen _____   6. China _____

3. Österreich _____   7. Slowenien _____

4. Türkei _____   8. Italien _____

Grammar

2. Fill in the correct form. It's the verb that's missing.

1. Gestern _____ ich frei.

2. Meine Schwester _____ auch Zeit.

3. Wir _____ in der Stadt.

4. Meine Schwester _____ das Auto.

5. Das _____ prima.

6. Um acht _____ wir wieder zu Hause.

3. Fill in the correct form. The personal pronoun is missing.

1. Wo ist mein Handy?   – Ich habe _____ nicht gesehen.

2. Wie findest du die CD?   – Ich finde _____ klasse.

3. Ich habe ein Problem.   – So? Was ist _____ denn?

4. Wie findest du meine Eltern?   – Ich finde _____ sehr sympathisch

5. Wie findest du meine Wohnung?   – Ich finde _____ nicht schlecht.

6. Besuchst du heute deine Geschwister? – Nein, ich habe _____ gestern besucht.

Check your answers in the key at the back of the book and then add up your points.

Total:	1 – 10	It would be a good idea to do this unit again straightaway.
	11 – 17	Pretty good. But it wouldn't hurt to go over the dialogues and the grammar again.
	18 – 20	Excellent. If you like, you could go over the vocabulary again, otherwise you can carry straight on.

Eine Mail von Robert – A mail from Robert

When Robert, Claudia and Niki are all back home in the evening, Robert writes an e-mail to his friend Jonas.

This lesson is all about jobs and professions. You'll also learn how to write letters and mails.

1 *Please match the professions.*
What do the people do for a living?

2 Robert writes an e-mail to his friend Jonas

Read the text. If you don't understand everything, don't worry. The main thing is that you find out what each of them does for a living.

→ *Listen and read.*
→ *Learn the vocabulary.*

herzliche Grüße	*best wishes*
Ich bin ein paar Tage bei Freunden.	*I'm staying with friends for a few days.*
Freund (der), die Freunde	*friend*
Ich glaube, du kennst sie.	*I think you know them.*
Heute haben wir die Familie von Claudia besucht.	*Today we visited Claudia's family.*
Claudias Vater ist Ingenieur.	*Claudia's father is an engineer.*
Er arbeitet als Controller.	*He works as a controller.*
Controller (der), die Controller	*controller*
Claudias Mutter ist Malerin.	*Claudia's mother is a painter.*
Malerin (die), die Malerinnen	*(woman) painter*
Sie arbeitet aber auch als Übersetzerin.	*But she also works as a translator.*
Übersetzerin (die), die Übersetzerinnen	*(woman) translator*
Claudias Bruder geht noch zur Schule.	*Claudia's brother is still at school.*
Er ist bald fertig.	*He'll soon be finished.*
bald	*soon*
fertig	*finished*
Regisseurin (die), die Regisseurinnen	*(female) director, producer*
Sie hat einen Film in Australien gemacht.	*She made a film in Australia.*
Film (der), die Filme	*film*
Australien	*Australia*
Für das Fernsehen.	*For television.*
Fernsehen (das)	*television*
Toll, was?	*Great, isn't it?*
toll	*great*
Was gibt's in München?	*What's on in Munich?*
Alles klar?	*Everything OK?*

3 *Answer the questions.*
Create your answers by putting the bits of the sentence into the right order.

In speech you can leave out the person and the verb if they have already occurred in the question. Then you get the following answers: *Bei Claudias Eltern. / Ingenieur. / Malerin. / Er geht noch zur Schule. / Katrin. / Interessant.*

4 *Claudia's family*
You'll find out more about the genitive in the grammar section.

5 *Robert is talking. Underline the correct form.*
You've already come across war *and* hatte. *In this text they occur again.*
Fill in the forms of sein. *Pay close attention to which sentence is in the past, and which is in the present.*

6 *Speaking exercise – First read the prompts.*
Listen to the question and answer as in the example. Then you'll hear the answer on the CD.

Someone would like to know what you do for a living. Use the suggestions we give you and choose the feminine or the masculine form. When you get to the fifth question, you can say what your real job is.

7 *Speaking exercise*
Answer as in the example. Then you'll hear the answer on the CD.

Again you're going to be asked about your job. This time your answer is more precise. Again you have to choose the feminine or masculine form.

8 *I write a mail.*
Write a mail home. Put the mail together from the text blocks that are given.

The genitive with proper nouns – Der Genitiv bei Eigennamen

Claudias Vater ist Controller. (= der Vater von Claudia)
Claudias Mutter ist Malerin. (= die Mutter von Claudia)

The genitive of proper nouns is formed as in English with *s*, but there is no apostrophe.
In speech people also use *von* + name: *die Mutter von Claudia.*

9 *How else can you say it?*
Imagine you're looking at some photos. You'll need these expressions. Transform the phrase
with von *into one with the genitive.*

Das ist die Mutter von Ralf. – Das ist _____ _____ .
Das sind die Eltern von Maxi. – Das sind _____ _____ .
Das ist der Bruder von Marie. – Das ist _____ _____ .
Das ist die Tochter von Frau Lehmann. – Das ist Frau _____ _____ .
Das ist der Sohn von Herrn Müller. – Das ist Herrn _____ _____ .
Das ist das Auto von Birgit. – Das ist _____ _____ .

10 *Match the right job names.*
We've selected a few jobs for you that didn't occur in the dialogues.

a. die Lehrerin

b. die Hausfrau

c. der Maurer

d. der Maler

e. der Frisör

f. die Verkäuferin

g. der Taxifahrer

_____

_____   _____   _____

Feminine job names – Feminine Berufsbezeichnungen

der Politiker, die Politiker	die Politiker**in**, die Politiker**innen**
der Student, die Studenten	die Student**in**, die Student**innen**
der Geschäftsmann, die Geschäftsleute	die Geschäfts**frau**, die Geschäfts**frauen**

The feminine form has the ending *-in*, plural *-innen*.
Careful: sometimes the vowel is changed into an
umlaut: *der Arzt, die Ärztin.*

11 *Fill in the missing forms.*
A lot of job titles for women end in -in (plural -innen). In the following table, either the male term or the female term is missing.

der	die	der	die
Regisseur		Informatiker	
	Malerin		Technikerin
Student		Lehrer	
Übersetzer			Schülerin
	Ingenieurin		Ärztin
	Frisörin		Taxifahrerin
Medien-Designer		Verkäufer	
Schornsteinfeger			Köchin
!!!	Hausfrau		Rechtsanwältin
Handwerker		Kfz-Mechaniker	
	Kellnerin		Redakteurin
Notarzt		Busfahrer	

12 *Revision*

Writing a personal mail

Hallo, … (+ Vorname)	*Hello/Hi …, (+ first name)*
Lieber/Liebe … (+ Vorname)	*Dear … (+ first name)*
Herzliche Grüße aus … (+ Stadt/Land)	*Best wishes from … (+ city/country)*
Bussi	*Kisses*

Jobs

arbeiten bei (Volkswagen) in (Wolfsburg) – er/sie arbeitet	*work for (Volkswagen) in (Wolfsburg)*
die Arbeit	*work*
das Büro, die Büros	*office*
das Gehalt, die Gehälter	*salary*
das Geschäft, die Geschäfte	*business, shop*
der Beruf, die Berufe	*job, profession*
der Job, die Jobs	*job*
der Stellenmarkt	*job market/situations vacant*
die Firma, die Firmen	*firm, company*
die Karriere, die Karrieren	*career*
die Stelle, die Stellen	*job/position*
verdienen – er/sie verdient, hat verdient	*earn*

13 *Listen carefully and repeat.*

Taxifahrer	Ich bin Taxifahrer	Ich bin Taxifahrerin.
Student	Ich bin Student.	Ich bin Studentin.
Schornsteinfeger	Ich bin Schornsteinfeger.	Ich bin Schornsteinfegerin.
Maurer	Ich bin Maurer.	
Verkäufer	Ich bin Verkäufer.	Ich bin Verkäuferin.
Übersetzer	Ich bin Übersetzer.	Ich bin Übersetzerin.

die Designerin	der Software-Entwickler
die Ärztin	der Informatiker
die Journalistin	der EDV-Kaufmann
die Stewardess	der Kfz-Mechaniker
die Architektin	der Ingenieur
die Sozialarbeiterin	der Maschinenbaumechaniker
die Bürokauffrau	der Polizist
die Bankkauffrau	der Elektroinstallateur
die Lehrerin	der Jounalist
die Rechtsanwältin	der Architekt

Cultural info (Textbook page 64)

Here are some job titles. You know all the terms already.
Careful: two jobs have only one form.

What's the job? Note down the masculine or feminine form too.

Statistics of dream jobs
The figures show the percentage of students interested in the following jobs listed.
You can listen to all the job titles in exercise 13 and repeat them.

Vocabulary

1. *Write the sentence.*

1. Franz | sein | Übersetzerin / Übersetzer _____
2. Ulrike | sein | Arzt / Ärztin _____
3. Tommy | sein | Taxifahrerin / Taxifahrer _____
4. Steffi | sein | Schüler / Schülerin _____
5. Frau Sommer | sein | Maler / Malerin _____
6. Herr Gruber | sein | Verkäufer / Verkäuferin _____

2. *Write the masculine or feminine form of the job title.*

1. der Politiker _____   4. die Verkäuferin _____
2. die Geschäftsfrau _____   5. der Student _____
3. der Arzt _____   6. der Ingenieur _____

Grammar

3. *Write the genitive:* Eva – Freund: Evas Freund.

1. Stefan | Vater _____   4. Anna | Tante _____
2. Filip | Schwester _____   5. Ulrike | Freundin _____
3. Frau Meier | Tochter _____   6. Katharina | Familie _____

4. *Write the plural.*

1. die Studentin _____   4. die Pilotin _____
2. die Ärztin _____   5. die Übersetzerin _____
3. die Freundin _____   6. die Politikerin _____

Listening Comprehension

2|42

5. *First listen to the dialogue. Then listen again and mark with a cross.*

1. Christine M. und Julia S.
☐ sind im Hotel.
☐ sind in der Firma.
☐ sind zu Hause.

2. Es ist
☐ noch früh.
☐ Mittag.
☐ Abend.

3. Sie frühstücken
☐ um acht Uhr.
☐ um halb acht.
☐ um acht Uhr fünfzehn.

4. Sie fahren
☐ eine halbe Stunde.
☐ eine dreiviertel Stunde.
☐ eine Stunde.

5. Sie haben einen Termin
☐ um neun Uhr.
☐ um halb neun.
☐ um zehn.

Check your answers in the key at the back of the book and then add up your points.

Total:		
	1 – 15	Oh dear, that's a pity. Please do this unit again.
	16 – 25	Not so bad. But even so, it would be a good idea to go over the dialogue and the grammar again.
	26 – 29	Excellent. There's nothing to stop you carrying on.

Some study tips:

1. Do the first lesson and time how long you need. The lessons are all roughly the same length, so this will tell you how much time you should plan for each lesson.
2. Try and set aside half an hour a day for studying. That is more effective than, for example, doing two or three hours at the weekend.
3. Make a point of listening to the texts and speaking exercises on the CDs over and over again (pictograms in the Workbook). This is a sure way of getting your ear accustomed to the sound of the language and the sentences. Repeat the pronunciation exercises as often as you can.
4. Buy a German newspaper or magazine from time to time. You'll soon discover words that you've learned and now know.
5. And most important of all: if you suddenly have the feeling that you're not making any progress, don't give up! As the proverb says, you can't expect to get everything right first time.

And now we've reached the end of the course. You've learned a lot of useful everyday language that you can use right away. And something about the German-speaking countries too. If you have time, come and visit us at: www.hueber.de. You'll find some information and tips on our homepage, and we'd like you to keep up your German and include it in your daily programme of study. Cheerio and see you soon!

Glossar – Glossary   German – English

Numbers refer to lessons

A

ab sofort	9	*immediately, with immediate effect*
Abend (der), -e	1	*evening*
Abendessen (das)	14	*supper, dinner*
abends	10	*in the evening(s)*
aber	2	*but*
Ach	2	*Oh*
Ach was!	8	*not at all, no*
Adieu	1	*(good)bye*
Adjektiv (das), -e	4	*adjective*
Adresse (die), -n	3	*address*
Aha.	3	*I see.*
Akkusativ (der), -e	11	*accusative*
alle	4	*all, everybody, everyone*
alles	12	*everything*
Alles bestens.	8	*Everything's fine. Just great.*
Alles klar?	15	*Everything OK?*
als (weiter als)	10	*than*
also	7	*right, so*
alt	6	*old*
Amerika (das)	14	*America*
an	15	*at, to*
Anmeldung (die), -en	12	*booking, reception*
anrufen – er/sie ruft an, hat angerufen	12	*phone, call*
Antwort (die), -en	2	*answer*
antworten – er/sie antwortet, hat geantwortet	2	*answer*
Anzeige (die), -n	9	*ad, advert*
Apfel (der), ⸚	8	*apple*
Appartement (das), -s: 1-Zimmer-Appartement	9	*flat, apartment: one-room flat/apartment*
Arbeit (die), -en	8	*work, job*
arbeiten (als ...) – er/sie arbeitet, hat gearbeitet	5, 15	*work (as ...)*
Architekt (der), -en/Architektin (die), -nen	15	*architect*
Archiv (das), -e	11	*filing room, archive*
Argentinien (das)	3	*Argentina*
Arm (der), -e	12	*arm*
Armbanduhr (die), -en	10	*watch*
Artikel (der), -	3	*article*
Arzt (der), ⸚e / Ärztin (die), -nen	15	*doctor*
Asien (das)	13	*Asia*
auch	1, 2	*too, also*
auf Deutsch	3	*in German*
Auf Wiederhören	7	*Goodbye [on the phone]*
Auf Wiedersehen/Auf Wiederschaun	1	*Goodbye*
Aufzug (der), ⸚e	11	*lift*

Auge (das), -n	12	*eye*
aus	2	*from, out of*
ausfüllen – er/sie füllt aus, hat ausgefüllt	3	*fill in*
Ausländer (der), -/Ausländerin (die), -nen	3	*foreigner*
Australien (das)	13	*Australia*
australisch	14	*Australian*
Ausweis-Nummer (die), -n	3	*identity card number*
Auto (das), -s: Auto fahren	2, 8	*car: to go by car*
Automat (der), -en	5	*machine*

B

Baby (das), -s	13	*baby*
Bad (das), ⸚er	9	*bath(room)*
baden – er/sie badet, hat gebadet	9	*(have a) bath; go swimming*
Bahn (die), -en	10	*railway, train*
Bahnhof (der), ⸚e	11	*station*
Bahnhofsuhr (die), -en	10	*station clock*
bald	15	*soon*
Balkon (der), -e	9	*balcony*
Bank (die), -en	12	*bank*
Bankkaufmann (der) ⸚er, -leute/Bankkauffrau (die), -en	15	*bank clerk*
Bauch (der), ⸚e	12	*stomach*
Bayern (das)	1	*Bavaria*
beantworten – er/sie beantwortet, hat beantwortet	6	*answer*
bedeuten – es/das bedeutet, hat bedeutet	3	*mean*
begrüßen – er/sie begrüßt, hat begrüßt	12	*greet*
bei + Dativ	6, 12	*for, at*
Bein (das), -e	12	*leg*
Beispiel (das), -e : zum Beispiel	6	*example: for example*
Belgien (das)	3	*Belgium*
Beruf (der), -e	6	*job, profession*
Berufsbezeichnung (die), -en	15	*job title*
besichtigen – er/sie besichtigt, hat besichtigt	12	*look around, see*
Besichtigung (die), -en	11	*guided tour*
besonders	6	*especially*
bestimmt	14	*definite(ly), certainly*
Besuch (der)	9	*visit*
besuchen – er/sie besucht, hat besucht	13	*visit*
betont	14	*stressed*
Bier (das), -e	14	*beer*
Bild (das), -er	13	*picture*
billig	11	*cheap*
bis (Mittag/morgen/...)	7	*till (noon/tomorrow/...)*
Bis gleich.	10	*See you soon/later.*
bitte	3	*please*
bitte (Danke – Bitte.)	5	*You're welcome*
Bitte sehr.	7	*Here you are.*
Bitte?	5	*Sorry?*
bleiben – er/sie bleibt, ist geblieben	9	*stay, remain*
Boutique (die), -n	12	*boutique*
Brasilien (das)	4	*Brazil*

brauchen – er/sie braucht, hat gebraucht	10	*need*
Braune (der) (= Kaffeesorte)	7	*brown coffee (sort of coffee)*
bringen – er/sie bringt, hat gebracht	9	*bring; take*
Brot (das), -e	13	*bread; sandwich*
Brötchen (das), -	13	*roll*
Bruder (der), ⸚	13	*brother*
Buchhaltung (die)	12	*accounts (department)*
Buchstabe (der), -n	7	*letter*
Buchstaben-Labyrinth (das), -e	11	*puzzle, maze*
Buchstabensalat (der), -e	8	*jumbled letters*
buchstabieren –er/sie buchstabiert, hat buchstabiert	3	*spell*
Bulgarien (das)	3	*Bulgaria*
Bundesland (das), ⸚er	5	*federal state*
Büro (das), -s	4	*office*
Bürokaufmann (der), ⸚er, -leute/Bürokauffrau (die), -en	15	*office clerk/administrator*
Bus (der), -se	11	*bus*
Busfahrer (der), -/Busfahrerin (die), -nen	15	*bus driver*
Bussi!	15	*kiss*
Butter (die)	13	*butter*
bzw. (= beziehungsweise)	15	*or*

C

Cappuccino (der) (= Kaffeesorte)	7	*cappuccino*
Casino (das), -s	12	*canteen*
CD (die), -s	15	*CD*
Chef (der), -s/Chefin (die), -nen	7	*boss*
China (das)	4	*China*
chinesisch	13	*Chinese*
Ciao	1	*cheers*
circa	12	*circa, approximately*
Controller (der), -/Controllerin, -nen	15	*controller*
Controlling (das)	12	*controlling (department)*
Cousin (der), -s/Cousine (die), -n	13	*(male) cousin; (female) cousin*

D

da	4	*here*
Dachwohnung (die), -en (das Dach + die Wohnung)	9	*penthouse*
danke	1	*thank you*
Danke/Danke sehr.	1, 5	*Thank you very much.*
dann	4	*then*
Das: Das bin/sind ...	1	*That: That is ...*
dass	12	*that*
Datum (das)	3	*date*
dauern – es dauert, hat gedauert	11	*last; take [time]*
dazu	9	*to it*
dein, deine	13	*your*
denn (Wie ist es denn in München?)	4	*So, ...*
Der Apfel fällt nicht weit vom Stamm.	8	*It's in the blood.*
Der Ton macht die Musik.	8	*It's the tone that makes the music.*
der, die, das	3	*the*

deshalb	13	*hence, thus, so*
Designer (der), - / Designerin (die), -nen	6	*designer*
deutsch	3	*German*
Deutschland (das)	1	*Germany*
Dialog (der), -e	3	*dialogue*
Dienstag (der)	7	*Tuesday*
Digitaluhr (die), -en	10	*digital watch*
direkt	4	*direct(ly)*
doch	12	*in fact*
Donnerstag (der)	12	*Thursday*
Doppelmokka (der) (= Kaffeesorte)	7	*double mocca*
dort	2	*there*
dran sein – er/sie ist dran, ist dran gewesen	8	*be someone's turn*
Dreiviertelstunde (die)	10	*three quarters of an hour*
du	1	*you*
durch (geteilt ...)	9	*by (divided ...)*
Durst (der): Durst haben	8	*thirst: be thirsty*

E

EDV-Fachmann (der), ̈er, -leute/EDV-Fachfrau (die), -en	15	*EDP-specialist*
Ei (das), -er	13	*egg*
Eigenname (der), -n	15	*proper noun*
eigentlich	13	*actually, in fact, really*
eilig	10	*in a hurry*
ein bisschen	1	*a bit*
ein paar	5	*a few*
ein/eine	7	*a*
Eindruck (der), ̈e	12	*impression*
Einfamilienhaus (das), ̈er	9	*(semi-)detached house (for one family)*
Eingang (der), ̈e	12	*entrance*
-einhalb	11	*and a half*
einige	9	*some, a few*
einladen – du lädst ein, er/sie lädt ein, hat eingeladen: zum Essen einladen	11	*invite: invite (s.o.) to dinner/lunch*
Eintrittskarte (die), -n	6	*ticket*
einverstanden	7	*OK, fine*
elegant	12	*elegant*
Elektroinstallateur (der), -e/Elektroinstallateurin (die), -nen	13	*electrician*
Eltern (die Pl)	13	*parents*
E-Mail (die), -s	3	*e-mail*
Empfang (der)	12	*reception*
endlich	13	*at last, finally*
Endung (die), -en	14	*ending*
England (das)	3	*England*
englisch	14	*English*
Enkel (der), -/Enkelin (die), -nen	13	*grandson/granddaughter*
Entschuldigen Sie ...	3	*Sorry ...*
Entschuldigung (die) ...	3	*Sorry ...*
er	1	*he*

Erdgeschoss (das), -e	12	*ground floor*
Erdteil (der), -e	11	*part of the world*
ergänzen – er/sie ergänzt, hat ergänzt	1	*complete*
erkennen – er/sie erkennt, hat erkannt	4	*recognise*
erzählen – er/sie erzählt, hat erzählt	12	*tell*
es (Personalpronomen)	3	*it*
es eilig haben – er/sie hat es eilig, hat es eilig gehabt	10	*be in a hurry*
es gibt (geben)	8	*there is, there are*
Es ist ... (1 Uhr)	10	*It is ... (1 o'clock)*
es: Wie geht es ...?	1	*How are/is ...?*
Espresso (der) (= Kaffeesorte)	7	*espresso (= sort of coffee)*
essen – du isst, er/sie isst, hat gegessen	8	*eat*
Essen (das), -	11	*meal, food, dinner*
essen gehen – er/sie geht essen, ist essen gegangen	8	*go out for a meal*
etwas	7	*something*
euer, eure	15	*your*
Euro (der), -s	5	*Euro*
Europa (das)	5	*Europe*
extra	8	*on purpose, specially*

F

fahren – du fährst, er/sie fährt, ist gefahren	5	*go, drive*
Fahrkarte (die), -n	5	*ticket*
Fahrt (die), -en	12	*trip, journey*
fallen – du fällst, er/sie fällt, ist gefallen	8	*fall*
falsch	4	*wrong*
falsch gehen (Uhr)	10	*be wrong (watch)*
Familie (die), -n	13	*family*
Familienname (der), -n	3	*surname, family name*
Familienstand (der)	3	*family status*
fast	10	*almost, nearly*
fehlen – es/das fehlt, hat gefehlt	6	*be missing*
feminin	7	*feminine*
Fernsehen (das)	15	*television*
fertig	15	*finished; ready*
Fest (das), -e	11	*special occasion, festival*
Fiaker (der) (= Kaffeesorte)	7	*Fiaker (= sort of coffee)*
Film (der), -e	14, 15	*film*
finden – er/sie findet, hat gefunden: eine Lösung finden	6, 12	*find; think: find a solution*
Firma (die), -en	7	*firm, company*
Firmenbesichtigung (die), -en	11	*(guided) tour of a company*
Firmenname (der), -n	6	*company name*
fliegen – er/sie fliegt, ist geflogen	11	*fly*
Fliegenpilz (der), -e (die Fliege + der Pilz)	9	*fly agaric*
Flughafen (der), ⸚	10	*airport*
Flugzeug (das), -e	11	*plane*
Flur (der), -e	9	*hall(way)*
Form (die), -en	12	*form, shape*
förmlich	12	*formal*

Formular (das), -e	3	*form*
Foto (das), -s	10	*photo*
Frage (die), -n	2	*question*
fragen – er/sie fragt, hat gefragt	2	*ask*
Fragewort (das), ⁼er	3	*question word*
Frankreich (das)	2	*France*
französisch	14	*French*
Frau (die), -en	1	*Mrs; wife; woman*
frei	9	*free; available*
Freitag (der)	12	*Friday*
Freund (der), -e/Freundin (die), -nen	12, 15	*friend, girlfriend*
freundlich	14	*friendly*
Frisör (= Friseur), -e/die Frisörin (= Friseurin), -nen	12, 15	*hairdresser*
früh	8	*early*
früher	8	*earlier, once*
Frühling (der)	13	*spring*
Frühstück (das)	13	*breakfast*
frühstücken – er/sie frühstückt, hat gefrühstückt	13	*have breakfast*
für + Akk.	9	*for*
furchtbar (... viel)	5	*terrible/terribly (a ... lot)*
Fuß (der), ⁼e	12	*foot*
Fußball (der)	6	*football*

G

Gabel (die), -n	13	*fork*
ganz	5, 13	*quite; very*
Garage (die), -n	9	*garage*
Garten (der), ⁼	9	*garden*
Gast (der), ⁼e	12	*visitor, guest*
Gäste-Casino (das)	12	*visitors' canteen*
geben – er/sie/es gibt, hat gegeben	7, 13	*there is, there are*
geboren sein (in)	3	*be born (in)*
Geburtsdatum (das), -daten	3	*date of birth*
Geburtsjahr (das), -e	3	*year of birth*
Geburtsland (das), ⁼er	3	*country of birth*
Geburtsname (der), -n	3	*maiden name*
Geburtsort (der), -e	3	*place of birth*
Geburtstag (der), -e	12	*birthday*
gefallen – du gefällst, er/sie gefällt, hat gefallen	14	*like*
gegen	14	*about*
gegenüber	12	*opposite*
Gehalt (das), ⁼er	9	*salary*
gehen – er/sie geht, ist gegangen	6, 7, 8	*go*
gehen – Wie geht's?	1	*How are you?*
Geld (das), -er	9	*money*
gemütlich	9	*cosy; comfortable*
Genitiv (der)	15	*genitive*
geöffnet (von ... bis ...)	12	*open (from ... to ...)*
geradeaus	11	*straight ahead/on*
gern, gerne	2, 4	*gladly; I'd like that.*
Geschäft (das), -e	1	*business; shop*

Geschäftsleben (das)	12	*business life*
Geschäftsleitung (die)	11	*management*
Geschäftsmann (der), ̈er, -leute/Geschäftsfrau (die), -en	6, 15	*businessman, businessmen/business-woman*
Geschäftspartner (der), -	12	*business partner*
Geschenk (das), -e	6	*present*
Geschichte (die)	6	*history*
geschieden	3	*divorced*
Geschlecht (das), -er	3	*gender*
geschlossen (Montag ...)	12	*shut, closed (Monday ...)*
Geschwister (die Pl)	13	*brothers and sisters*
Gespräch (das), -e	11	*conversation*
gestern	8	*yesterday*
gesund	12	*healthy, good for you*
Gesundheit (die)	12	*health*
glauben – er/sie glaubt, hat geglaubt	12	*believe, think*
gleich (=)	9	*equal*
gleich	10, 13	*in a minute, straightaway*
Glossar (das), -e	1	*glossary*
Glück (das): Glück bringen	1, 4, 5, 9	*luck*
GmbH (die), -s	3	*Ltd, PLC*
Grammatik (die)	1	*grammar*
Griechenland (das)	10	*Greece*
griechisch	14	*Greek*
groß	3, 5	*big, large, tall*
Großbritannien (das)	3	*Great Britain*
große Braune (der) (= Kaffeesorte)	7	*large brown (= sort of coffee)*
Großeltern (die Pl)	13	*grandparents*
Großmutter (die), ̈/ Großvater (der), ̈	13	*grandmother/grandfather*
Großstadt (die), ̈e	5	*city*
Gruß (der), ̈e	12	*greeting*
Grüß Gott/Grüezi/Griaß di	1	*Hello*
gut	1	*good*
Gute Nacht	1	*Good night*
Guten Abend	1	*Good evening*
Guten Morgen	1	*Good morning*
Guten Tag	1	*Hello: Good morning/afternoon*

H

Haar (das), -e	12	*hair*
haben – er/sie hat, hat gehabt	4, 8	*have*
Hafen (der), ̈	10	*docks, harbor, port*
halb (... drei)	10	*half*
halbe Stunde (die): eine halbe (1/2) Stunde	10	*half an hour*
Hallo	1	*hello; hi*
Hals (der), ̈e	12	*neck*
Haltestelle (die), -n	13	*stop*
Hand (die), ̈e: sich die Hand/Hände schütteln	12	*hand: shake hands*
Handwerker (der), - /Handwerkerin (die), -nen	15	*tradesman, craftsman/tradeswoman, craftswoman*
Handy (das), -s	6	*mobile (phone)*

Handy-Nummer (die), -n	6	*mobile number*
hässlich	12	*ugly*
Hauptstadt (die), ⸚e	10	*capital (city)*
Haus (das), ⸚er: zu Hause	5, 8	*house, building: at home*
Hausfrau (die), -en/Hausmann (der), ⸚er	13	*housewife; house husband*
Hausnummer (die), -n	11	*house number*
heißen – er/sie heißt	1	*to be called*
heißen: das heißt	11	*that is, actually*
helfen – du hilfst, er/sie hilft, hat geholfen	7	*help*
Herr (der), -en	1	*Mr*
Herstellung (die)	12	*production (department)*
herzlich	1	*warm; hearty*
Herzlich willkommen	1	*welcome*
herzliche Grüße (aus)	15	*best wishes (from)*
heute	5	*today*
heute Abend/Mittag	10, 11	*this evening*
hier	4	*here*
Hilfe (die), -n: Hilfe!	12	*help: Help!*
Hobby (das), -s	6	*hobby*
hoffen – er/sie hofft, hat gehofft	12	*hope*
höflich	7	*polite*
Holland (das)	14	*Holland*
holländisch	14	*Dutch*
hören – er/sie hört, hat gehört	1	*hear; listen to*
Hotel (das), -s	3	*hotel*
Hotelanmeldung (die), -en	3	*hotel registration (form)*
Hotelzimmer (das), -	10	*hotel room*
Hufeisen (das), -	9	*horseshoe*
Hunger (der): Hunger haben	8	*hunger: be hungry*

I

ich	1	*I*
ihr	1	*you (plural)*
ihr, ihre	6	*her, your*
im Norden/Süden von …	9	*to the north/south of …*
immer	6	*always*
in	2	*in*
„in" sein	12	*be "in"*
in der Nähe	13	*nearby*
Indien (das)	3	*India*
Indonesien (das)	3	*Indonesia*
Informatik (die)	6	*computer science*
Informatiker (der), -/Informatikerin (die), -nen	7	*computer scientist*
Information (die), -en	11	*information*
Informationszentrum (das), -zentren	12	*information centre*
informell	10	*informal*
Ingenieur (der), -e/Ingenieurin (die), -nen	6, 15	*engineer*
Inhalt (der), -e	1	*contents*
interessant	9	*interesting*
Interview (das), -s	4	*interview*
Irak (der/-)	3	*Iraq*

Iran (der/-)	3	*Iran*
irisch	14	*Irish*
IT-Abteilung (die), -en	12	*IT department*
Italien (das)	2	*Italy*
italienisch	14	*Italian*

J

ja	1	*yes*
Ja/Nein-Frage (die), -n	4	*yes/no-question*
ja: Sie sind ja ...	4	*yes, indeed, in fact; In fact you are ...*
Jahr (das), -e	2	*year*
Jahreszeit (die), -en	13	*season*
Japan (das)	3	*Japan*
japanisch	14	*Japanese*
jemand	8	*somebody*
Jemen (der)	3	*Yemen*
jetzt	7	*now*
Job (der), -s	3	*job*
Journalist (der), -en/Journalistin (die), -nen	15	*journalist*
Junge (der), -n	13	*boy*

K

Kaffee (der), -s	7	*coffee*
Kaffeepause (die), -n	7	*coffee break*
Kalender (der), -	12	*calendar*
kalt	4	*cold*
Kanal (der), ⸚e	10	*canal, channel*
Kantine (die), -n	7	*canteen*
Kantinenleitung (die)	12	*canteen manager*
kaputt	11	*broken*
Kapuziner (der), (= Kaffeesorte)	7	*Kapuziner (= sort of coffee)*
Karriere (die), -n	6	*career*
Karte (die), -n	3, 5, 7	*map*
Käse (der)	13	*cheese*
kein, keine	11	*no*
Keller (der), -	11	*cellar, basement*
kennen – er/sie kennt, hat gekannt	2	*know*
kennenlernen – er/sie lernt kennen, hat kennengelernt	12	*get to know*
Kfz-Mechaniker (der), - /Kfz-Mechanikerin (die), -nen (Kfz = Kraftfahrzeug)	15	*mechanic*
Kilometer (der), -	6	*kilometre*
Kind (das), -er	13	*child*
klar	2	*of course [lit: clear]*
klasse	8	*great*
Kleeblatt (das), ⸚er	9	*cloverleaf*
klein	5	*small, little*
kleine Braune (der) (= Kaffeesorte)	7	*small brown (= sort of coffee)*
Kleinstadt (die), ⸚e	5	*small town*
kochen – er/sie kocht, hat gekocht	8	*cook*
Kollege (der), -n	12	*colleague*

kommen – er/sie kommt, ist gekommen	2, 11	come
Kommt Zeit, kommt Rat.	8	Take your time and you'll find an answer.
Konferenzraum (der), ¨e	12	conference room
Konferenzzimmer (das), -	12	conference room
können – er/sie kann	7	can, be able to
Kontinent (der), -e	13	continent
Kopf (der), ¨e	12	head
Korea (das)	4	Korea
Koreaner (der), -/Koreanerin (die), -nen	4	Korean (man/woman)
korrigieren – er/sie korrigiert, hat korrigiert	5	correct
kosten	5	cost
krank	12	ill
Krankenzimmer (das), -	12	sickbay
Krankheit (die), -en	12	illness, disease
Küche (die), -n	9	kitchen; cuisine
Küchenuhr (die), -en	10	kitchen clock
Kuckucksuhr (die), -en	10	cuckoo clock
kurz	5	brief, (in) short

L

Lager (das), -	12	warehouse, stockroom
Land (das), ¨er	3	country
Ländername (der), -n	3	name of a country
Landkarte (die), -n	5	map
lang, lange	5	for a long time
lang: der lange Vokal	2	long: long vowel
langsam	3	slow(ly)
leben – er/sie lebt, hat gelebt	2	live
ledig	3	single
Lehrer (der), -/Lehrerin (die), -nen	15	teacher
leider	4	unfortunately, I'm afraid
Leiter (der), -	4	head
Leitung (die), -en	12	management
Lektion (die), -en	1	lesson
lernen – er/sie lernt, hat gelernt	14	learn
lesen – du liest, er/sie liest, hat gelesen	5	read
Lettland (das)	7	Latvia
Libanon (der)	3	Lebanon
Liebe Grüße	15	Love (from)
lieber (als) (gern – lieber – am liebsten)	13	like more (than) (like – like more – like most)
Lieber .../Liebe ...	15	Dear ...
Lieblings- (-essen/-bruder/-film/-hotel ...)	14	favourite (meal ...)
liegen - es liegt	6	to be located
Likör (der)	8	liqueur
Limo (die), -s (= Limonade (die), -en)	8	lemonade
links	12	left
Liter (= l) (der)	7	litre
Löffel (der), -	13	spoon
Lösung (die), -en	9	solution

M

machen – er/sie macht, hat gemacht	8	*make, do*
machen: Das macht nichts.	7	*That's OK/all right./That doesn't matter.*
macht nichts (= Das ...)	10	*that's OK/all right*
Mädchen (das), -	13	*girl*
Mahlzeit (die)	12	*hello (greeting among colleagues in the middle of the day)*
Mail (die), -s	15	*email*
mal: Sag mal ...	13	*Tell me ...*
Maler (der), -/Malerin (die), -nen	15	*painter*
Mama (die)	14	*mum(my)*
man	8	*one; you; people*
manchmal	12	*sometimes*
Mann (der), ¨er	13	*man; husband*
männlich	3	*male*
Marienkäfer (der), - (der Käfer)	9	*ladybird (beetle)*
Marketing (das)	7	*marketing*
Marketing-Abteilung (die), -en	12	*marketing (department)*
Marketing-Chef (der)	7	*head of marketing*
markieren – er/sie markiert, hat markiert	1	*mark*
Markt (der), ¨e	12	*market*
Marmelade (die), -n	13	*jam*
Maschinenbaumechaniker (der), - /Maschinenbaumechanikerin (die), -nen	15	*mechanic, engineer*
maskulin	7	*masculine*
Maurer (der), -/ Maurerin (die), -nen	13	*bricklayer*
Medien-Design	6	*media design*
Medien-Designer (der), -/Medien-Designerin (die), -nen	6	*media designer*
mein, meine	1, 13	*my*
meinen – er/sie meint, hat gemeint	13	*think*
meistens	12	*usually, mostly*
Melange (die) (= Kaffeesorte)	7	*Melange (= sort of coffee)*
Messer (das), -	13	*knife*
Meter (der/das), -	9	*metre*
mexikanisch	14	*Mexican*
Mexiko	14	*Mexico*
Miete (die), -n	9	*rent*
mieten – er/sie mietet, hat gemietet	11	*rent*
Milch (die)	7	*milk*
Milchkaffee (der), -s	7	*milky coffee, coffee with milk*
Million (die), -en	6	*million*
minus	9	*minus*
Minute (die), -n	5	*minute*
mit + Dat.	3, 5, 11	*with*
mitkommen – er/sie kommt mit, ist mitgekommen	13	*come along, come with someone*
Mittag (der), -e	7	*lunchtime, midday*
mittags	10	*at lunchtime*
Mittwoch (der)	12	*Wednesday*
möchten – er/sie möchte	7	*would like*

mögen – er/sie mag, hat gemocht	13	*like*
Mokka (der), (= Kaffeesorte)	7	*mocca (= sort of coffee)*
Moldawien (das)	3	*Moldavia*
Moment (der), -e (einen Moment ...; im Moment)	11	*moment: just a moment ...; at the moment*
Monat (der), -e	3	*month*
monatlich	9	*monthly*
monatlich kalt/warm	9	*basic rent without heating/including heating*
Montag (der)	12	*Monday*
morgen	4	*tomorrow*
Morgen (der), -	1	*morning*
morgens	10	*in the morning*
Mund (der), ⸚er	12	*mouth*
mündlich	10	*oral(ly)*
Musik (die)	6	*music*
Müsli (das)	13	*muesli*
Mutter (die), ⸚	13	*mother*

N

Na ja	2	*well*
na klar	8	*of course*
nach	5, 10	*to*
nach Hause	5	*home*
nach: nach rechts	12	*to: to the right*
Nachbarland (das), ⸚er	5	*neighbouring country*
nachgehen: die Uhr geht nach, ist nachgegangen	10	*lose: the watch is slow*
nachmittags	10	*in the afternoon(s)*
Nachname (der), -n	1	*last name, surname*
nachsprechen – du sprichst nach, er/sie spricht nach, hat nachgesprochen	13	*repeat*
Nacht (die), ⸚e: Gute Nacht	1	*night: Good night*
Nähe (die)	13	*proximity*
Name (der), -n	3	*name*
nämlich	8	*namely, in fact*
Nationalität (die), -en	3	*nationality*
natürlich	7	*of course*
negativ	4	*negative*
nehmen – du nimmst, er/sie nimmt, hat genommen	7	*take*
Nein	3	*No*
nett	5	*nice*
neu	3, 6	*new*
Neuseeland (das)	4	*New Zealand*
neutral	7	*neuter*
nicht	2	*not*
nicht wahr?	14	*don't you?*
nichts	7	*nothing*
nie	12	*never*
Niederlande (die Pl)	2	*Netherlands*
niemand	8	*nobody*
noch	5	*still*

noch einmal	5	*once again*
Nomen (das), -	3	*noun*
Nominativ (der), -e	9	*nominative*
Norddeutschland (das)	1	*Northern Germany*
Norden (der)	6	*north*
Nordeuropa (das)	7	*Northern Europe*
nördlich (von)	6	*north (of)*
Norwegen (das)	10	*Norway*
Notarzt (der), ⸚e/Notärztin (die), -nen	12	*emergency doctor*
notieren – er/sie notiert, hat notiert	5	*note (down)*
Notiz (die), -en: Notizen machen	7	*note*
null (= 0)	9	*zero*
Nummer (die), -n	3	*number*
nur	7	*only*

O

Oberbegriff (der), -e	13	*generic term*
Obst (das)	13	*fruit*
oder	1	*or*
offiziell	10	*official(ly)*
öffnen – er/sie öffnet, hat geöffnet	12	*open*
Öffnungszeiten (die Pl)	12	*opening times/hours*
oft	12	*often*
ohne + Akk.	2	*without*
Oma (die), -s	13	*grandma*
Onkel (der), -s	13	*uncle*
Opa (der), -s	13	*grandpa*
Ordnung (die): in Ordnung	11	*OK: in order*
Ort (der), -e	3	*place*
Osten (der)	6	*east*
Österreich (das)	1	*Austria*
östlich (von)	6	*east (of)*

P

Papa (der), -s	14	*daddy*
Party (die), -s	6	*party*
Pass (der), ⸚e	3	*passport*
passen – es passt, hat gepasst	1	*fit*
passend	2	*suitable, fitting*
passieren – es/das passiert, ist passiert	12	*happen*
Pass-Nummer (die), -n	3	*passport number*
Passwort (das), ⸚er	11	*password*
Pause (die), -n	7	*break, pause*
Pension (die), -en	11	*boarding house*
perfekt	14	*perfect(ly)*
Person (die), -en	1	*person*
Personalpronomen (das), -	4	*personal pronoun*
Pfiat di	1	*cheers*
Pilot (der), -en/Pilotin (die), -nen	15	*pilot*
Plakat (das), -e	12	*poster*

Platz (der), ⁝e: viel/wenig Platz; Platz nehmen; Platz machen	3, 9, 12	*place: a lot of/little space; sit down, take a seat; make room*
plötzlich	12	*sudden(ly)*
Plural (der), -e	1	*plural*
plus	9	*plus*
Polen (das)	3	*Poland*
Politiker (der), -/Politikerin (die), -nen	15	*politician*
Polizist (der), -en/Polizistin (die), -nen	15	*police officer*
Portugal (das)	10	*Portugal*
positiv	4	*positive*
Possessivartikel (der), -	13	*possessive article*
Postleitzahl (= PLZ) (die), -en	3	*postcode, zipcode*
praktisch	4	*practical, handy*
Präsens (das)	2	*present*
Präteritum (das)	14	*past*
Praxis (die), Praxen	12	*practice, surgery*
prima	4	*great, fantastic*
pro (pro Person)	9	*per (per person)*
probieren – er/sie probiert, hat probiert	8	*try (out)*
Probieren geht über studieren.	8	*The proof of the pudding is in the eating.*
Problem (das), -e; Kein Problem.	10	*problem; No problem.*
Produktion (die), -en	12	*production (department)*
Pünktlichkeit (die)	12	*punctuality*

Q

qm = m2 (= Quadratmeter)	9	*sq.m. (= square metre)*
Quittung (die), -en	10	*receipt*
Quiz (das)	2	*quiz*

R

Rätsel (das), -	9	*puzzle*
Raum (der), ⁝e	12	*room, space*
rechnen – er/sie rechnet, hat gerechnet	9	*do sums, calculate*
recht haben – er/sie hat recht, hat recht gehabt	8	*be right*
rechts	12	*(on the) right*
Rechtsanwalt (der), ⁝e/Rechtsanwältin (die), -nen	15	*lawyer, attorney*
Redaktion (die), -en	12	*editorial (department)*
Regisseur (der), -e/Regisseurin (die), -nen	13	*director, producer*
regnen – es regnet, hat geregnet	4	*rain*
reichen – es/das reicht, hat gereicht	9	*be enough*
Reise (die), -n	4	*journey, trip, travel*
Reiseziel (das), -e	10	*destination*
Reporter (der), -	3	*reporter*
Restaurant (das), -s	13	*restaurant*
richtig	2	*correct*
richtig gehen: die Uhr geht richtig, ist richtig gegangen	10	*be right: the watch/clock is right*
rufen – er/sie ruft, hat gerufen	12	*call*
Rumänien (das)	3	*Romania*
Russland (das)	3	*Russia*

S

German	Ref	English
sagen – er/sie sagt, hat gesagt: sagt man	2, 8	*say, tell: people say*
Salat (der), -e	8	*salad*
Salut	1	*bye*
Satz (der), ¨e	3	*sentence*
Satzstellung (die), -en	12	*word order*
S-Bahn (die) (S = schnell), -en	5	*S-Bahn; city and suburban railway*
schade	8	*pity*
Schale (die), -n (= Kaffeetasse)	7	*bowl (= coffee cup)*
scheinen – er/sie scheint, hat geschienen	4	*shine; seem*
schlafen – du schläfst, er/sie schläft, hat geschlafen	9	*sleep*
Schlafzimmer (das), -	9	*bedroom*
schlecht	4	*bad(ly)*
schlimm	5	*bad(ly)*
Schloss (das), ¨er	6	*castle*
Schmerzen (die Pl)	12	*pain, ache*
schneien – es schneit, hat geschneit	4	*snow*
schnell	3	*quick(ly), fast*
schon	2	*already*
schön	4	*nice, pretty, beautiful*
Schornsteinfeger (der), - / Schornsteinfegerin (die), -nen	9, 15	*chimney sweep*
schrecklich	10	*awful(ly), terrible/terribly*
schreiben – er/sie schreibt, hat geschrieben	1	*write*
Schule (die), -n	13	*school*
Schüler (der), -/Schülerin (die), -nen	15	*schoolboy/-girl*
schütteln sich die Hand – er/sie schüttelt, hat geschüttelt: sich die Hand schütteln	12	*shake hands*
Schwarze (der), (= Kaffeesorte)	7	*black (= sort of coffee)*
Schweden (das)	10	*Sweden*
Schwein (das), -e	9	*pig; pork*
Schweiz (die)	1	*Switzerland*
schweizerisch	14	*Swiss*
schwer	6	*difficult; heavy*
Schwester (die), -n	13	*sister*
Schwiegersohn (der), ¨e/Schwiegertochter (die), ¨	13	*son-in-law/daughter-in-law*
Schwiegervater (der), ¨/Schwiegermutter (die), ¨	13	*father-in-law/mother-in-law*
sehen – du siehst, er/sie sieht, hat gesehen	10	*see*
sehr	2	*very (much)*
sein – er/sie ist, ist gewesen	1	*be*
sein, seine	6	*his, its*
Seite (die), -n	2	*side; page*
Sekretariat (das), -e	11	*secretary's office*
Selbstbedienung (die)	12	*self-service*
Semesterferien (die Pl)	13, 14	*(university) vacation*
senkrecht	7	*vertical(ly); down (in crossword)*
Serviette (die), -n	7	*serviette, napkin*
Servus	1	*bye*
sich die Hand schütteln – sie schütteln sich die Hand, haben sich die Hand geschüttelt	12	*shake hands*

sich entschuldigen – er/sie entschuldigt sich, hat sich entschuldigt	12	*apologise*
sich ergeben – es/das ergibt sich, hat sich ergeben	11	*make (up)*
sich sehen – sie sehen sich, haben sich gesehen	12	*meet*
sicher	14	*certain(ly), definite(ly)*
sie (Pl)	1	*they*
sie (Sg)	1	*she*
Sie (Sg/Pl)	1	*you (formal)*
Silbe (die), -n	11	*syllable*
Singular (der)	1	*singular*
sitzen – er/sie sitzt, hat gesessen	12	*sit*
Ski fahren – du fährst Ski, er/sie fährt Ski, ist Ski gefahren	6	*ski, go skiing*
Skizze (die), -n	12	*sketch*
Slowenien (das)	3	*Slovenia*
so	2	*so*
so gegen ...	14	*about ...*
sofort	9	*at once, immediately*
Software-Entwickler (der), -/Software-Entwicklerin (die), -nen	15	*software developer*
sogar	9	*even*
Sohn (der), ⸚e	13	*son*
Sommer (der)	13	*summer*
Sonnabend/Samstag (der)	12	*Saturday*
Sonne (die)	4	*sun*
Sonntag (der), -e	12	*Sunday*
Sorgen (die Pl)	8	*worries*
Sozialarbeiter (der), -/Sozialarbeiterin (die), -nen	15	*social worker*
Spaghetti (die Pl)	8	*spaghetti*
Spanien (das)	3	*Spain*
spanisch	14	*Spanish*
sparen – er/sie spart, hat gespart	9	*save*
Spargel (der), -	14	*asparagus*
Spaß (der): Spaß machen	8	*fun: be fun*
spät	5	*late*
später	8	*later*
Sprache (die), -n	6	*language*
Sprachenschule (die), -n	14	*language school*
sprechen – du sprichst, er/sie spricht, hat gesprochen	3, 8, 14	*speak*
Sprechstunde (die), -n	12	*surgery*
Sprechübung (die), -en	10	*speaking exercise*
Sprichwort (das), ⸚er	8	*proverb*
Stadt (die), ⸚e	3	*town, city*
Stadtautobahn (die), -en	10	*urban motorway/freeway*
Städtename (der), -n	2	*name of a town/city*
Stadtplan (der), ⸚e	12	*town/city map*
Stadtrundfahrt (die), -en	4	*town/city tour*
Start (der), -s	3	*start*
starten – er/sie startet, ist gestartet	11	*start, set off, take off*
Stau (der), -s	10	*traffic jam, tailback*

Stelle (die), -n	15	job
Stellenmarkt (der), ⁼e	15	job market; situations vacant
Steward (der), -s/Stewardess (die), -en	6, 15	steward/stewardess
Stichwort (das), ⁼er	13	note, entry, headword, keyword
stimmen – es/das stimmt, hat gestimmt	8	be right
Straße (die), -n	3	street; road
Student (der), -en/Studentin (die), -nen	6	student
studieren – er/sie studiert, hat studiert	6	study
Stunde (die), -n	5, 10	hour
suchen – er/sie sucht, hat gesucht	2	look for
Sudan (der)	3	Sudan
Süden (der)	6	south
südlich (von)	6	south (of)
super	5	super
Supermarkt (der), ⁼e	12	supermarket
sympathisch	6	nice

T

Tag (der), -e	1	day
Tagebuch (das). ⁼er	8	diary
täglich	12	daily
Tante (die), -n	13	aunt
Taschenuhr (die), -en	10	pocket watch
Tasse (die), -n	7	cup
Taxi (das), -s	10	taxi
Taxifahrer (der), -/Taxifahrerin (die), -nen	10, 15	taxi driver
Techniker (der), -/Technikerin (die), -nen	15	technician
Tee (der), -s	7	tea
Teil (der), -e	11	part
Tel./Telefon (das)	3	(tele)phone
telefonieren – er/sie telefoniert, hat telefoniert	7	(tele)phone, make a phone call
Telefonnummer (die), -n	6	(tele)phone number
Teller (der), -	13	plate
Tennis (das)	6	tennis
Termin (der), -e	10	appointment
Terrasse (die), -n	9	terrace, patio
Test (der), -s	13	test
teuer	11	expensive
Text (der), -e	5	text
Textbaustein (der), -e	15	text block
Textbuch (das), ⁼er	1	textbook
Ticket (das), -s	6	ticket
Tipp (der), -s	12	tip
Tochter (die), ⁼	13	daughter
Toilette (die), -n	9	toilet
toll	14	great
Ton (der), ⁼e	8	tone
Tourist (der), -en	12	tourist
Traumberuf (der), -e	15	dream job
träumen – er/sie träumt, hat geträumt	10	dream
Treppe (die), -n	12	stairs, staircase

trinken – er/sie trinkt, hat getrunken	7	*drink*
Tschüs	1	*bye; cheers*
tun – er/sie tut, hat getan	12	*do; put*
Tür (die), -en	9	*door*
Türkei (die)	3	*Turkey*
türkisch	14	*Turkish*
Tut mir leid.	7	*I'm sorry.*

U

üben – er/sie übt, hat geübt	11	*practise*
Überraschung (die), -en	8	*surprise*
übersetzen – er/sie übersetzt, hat übersetzt	15	*translate*
Übersetzer (der), - /Übersetzerin (die), -nen	15	*translator*
Übersetzung (die), -en	12	*translation*
übrigens	13	*by the way*
Übung (die), -en	1	*exercise*
Uf Widerluege	1	*goodbye*
Uhr (die), -en: Es ist 6 Uhr.	10	*clock, o'clock: It's 6 o'clock*
Uhrzeit (die), -en	10	*time*
um (…6 Uhr)	10	*at (… 6 o'clock)*
unbestimmt	7	*indefinite*
und	1	*and*
ungefähr	10	*about, roughly*
Uni (= Universität) (die), -s	12	*uni (= university)*
Universität (die), -en	7	*university*
unpünktlich	12	*unpunctual*
Unterschrift (die), -en	3	*signature*
unterstreichen – er/sie unterstreicht, hat unterstrichen	1	*underline*
USA (die Vereinigten Staaten von Amerika)	3	*USA*
usw. (= und so weiter)	3	*etc.*

V

Vater (der), ⸚	13	*father*
Verb (das), -en	2	*verb*
verboten	6	*forbidden*
verdienen – er/sie verdient, hat verdient	15	*earn, deserve*
vergleichen – er/sie vergleicht, hat verglichen	1	*compare*
verheiratet	3	*married*
Verkäufer (der) -/die Verkäuferin, -nen	15	*(shop) assistant*
Verkehr (der)	10	*traffic*
Verneinung (die)	4	*negation*
Versand (der)	12	*despatch (department)*
verstehen – er/sie versteht, hat verstanden	12	*understand*
Vertrieb (der)	11	*sales (department)*
Viel Glück!	13	*Good luck!*
Viel Spaß!	11	*Have a good time!/Enjoy yourself/yourselves!*
viel, viele	5	*much, many*
viele Grüße (aus …)	15	*best wishes (from …)*
Vielen Dank	5	*Thank you very much*

vielleicht	4	*perhaps, maybe*
Viertel vor/nach ..., viertel ...	10	*a quarter (to/past ...)*
Viertelstunde (die)	10	*quarter of an hour*
Visitenkarte (die), -n	3	*business card*
Visum (das), Visa	3	*visa*
Vokal (der), -e	8	*vowel*
Vokalwechsel (der), -	8	*vowel change*
Volkswagen (der), -	15	*Volkswagen*
von ... bis	12	*from ... till*
von + Dativ	3	*of, from*
von Beruf (sein)	6	*by profession, work as a ...*
Von nichts kommt nichts. (Sprichwort)	8	*You don't get anything without effort. (Proverb)*
vor (... 6 Uhr)	10	*to (... 6 o'clock)*
vor/nach (Minuten)	10	*to/past (minutes)*
vorgehen: die Uhr geht vor, ist vorgegangen	10	*be fast: the clock is fast*
Vormittag (der)	12	*morning*
vormittags	10	*in the morning(s)*
Vorname (der), -n	3	*first name*
Vorschlag (der), ⁼e	11	*suggestion*
Vorwahlnummer (die), -n	11	*dialling code, area code*
Vorwort (das)	1	*foreword, introduction*

W

waagerecht	7	*horizontal; across (in crossword)*
Wagen (der), -	14	*car*
Wann?	5	*When?*
warm	4	*warm*
warten – er/sie wartet, hat gewartet	11	*wait*
Warum?	11	*Why?*
was = etwas	8	*something*
Was?	3	*What?*
Wasser (das)	10	*water*
WC (das), -s	9	*WC*
Weg (der), -e	11	*way, path*
weg sein – er/sie ist weg, ist weg gewesen	13	*be away, be gone*
wehtun – es/das tut weh, hat weh getan	12	*hurt*
weiblich	3	*female*
weiß	14	*white*
weit	4	*far, a long way*
Welcher?/Welche?/Welches?	5	*What? Which?*
wenig, wenige	5	*little, few*
wenn	12	*when*
Wer Sorgen hat, hat auch Likör.	8	*He who has worries also has liqueur.*
Wer?	6	*Who?*
werden – du wirst, er/sie wird, ist geworden	12	*become*
Westen (der)	6	*west*
westlich (von)	6	*west (of)*
Wetter (das)	4	*weather*
W-Frage (die), -n	6	*wh-questions*
wichtig	12	*important*

wie (A wie Anton)	6	*as (A for/as in Anton)*
Wie alt?	6	*How old?*
Wie bitte?	5	*Sorry?*
Wie lange?	5	*How long?*
Wie spät (ist es)?	10	*What's the time?*
Wie weit?	10	*How far?*
Wie?	1	*How? What?*
wieder	5	*again*
wiederholen – er/sie wiederholt, hat wiederholt	3	*repeat*
Wiener Melange (die) (= Kaffeesorte)	7	*Viennese Melange (= sort of coffee)*
willkommen	1	*welcome*
windig	4	*windy*
wir	1	*we*
wirklich	14	*really*
Wo?	2	*Where?*
Woche (die), -n	13	*week*
Wochenende (das), -n	13	*weekend*
Wochentag (der), -e	12	*day of the week*
Woher?	2	*Where from?*
Wohin?	8	*Where to?*
wohnen – er/sie wohnt, hat gewohnt	2	*live*
Wohnung (die), -en	9	*flat*
Wohnzimmer (das), -	9	*living room*
Wort (das), ¨er	5	*word*
Wörtersalat (der)	13	*jumbled words*

Z

Zahl (die), -en	3	*number*
Zahn (der), ¨e	12	*tooth*
Zahnschmerzen (die Pl)	12	*toothache*
zeichnen – er/sie zeichnet, hat gezeichnet	12	*draw*
zeigt: die Uhr zeigt	10	*the clock shows*
Zeit (die), -en	4	*time*
Zeit (die): Zeit haben	4, 6	*time: have time*
Zeitangabe (die), -n	11	*time*
Zeitschrift (die), -en	12	*magazine*
Zentrum (das), Zentren	4	*centre*
Ziel (das), -e	3	*destination; goal, target*
ziemlich	15	*fairly, quite*
Zimmer (das), -	9	*room*
zu (spät)	12	*too (late)*
zu Fuß (gehen)	12	*on foot (walk)*
zu Hause	8	*at home*
zu spät: zu spät kommen	10	*too late: be late*
zu/zum/zur + Dativ	10, 11	*to*
Zucker (der)	7	*sugar*
zuerst	4	*(at) first*
Zug (der), ¨e	11	*train*
zuhören – er/sie hört zu, hat zugehört	3	*listen*
zum Glück	12	*luckily, fortunately*
zum Schluss	14	*at the end, finally*

zum/zur: zur Schule gehen	10, 13	*to the: go to school*
Zuname (der), -n	6	*surname*
zuordnen – er/sie ordnet zu, hat zugeordnet	1	*match*
zurück	11	*back*
zurückfahren – er/sie fährt zurück, ist zurückgefahren	12	*drive/go back*
zurückfliegen – er/sie fliegt zurück, ist zurückgeflogen	11	*fly back*
zurückgehen – er/sie geht zurück, ist zurückgegangen	12	*go back*
zusammengehören – es/das gehört zusammen, hat zusammengehört	3	*belong together*
zusammenpassen – das passt zusammen, hat zusammengepasst	1	*go together, fit*
zusammensetzen – er/sie setzt zusammen, hat zusammengesetzt	15	*put together*
zwischen + Dativ	14	*between*

Lösungen / Key to the exercises

Lesson 1

1 a3, b4, c1, d2, e5

3 Guten Tag. Sind Sie Herr Heinrich? / Ja, das bin ich. / Mein Name ist Bruckner, Chris Bruckner. / Guten Tag, Frau Bruckner. Herzlich willkommen.
Hallo, Rob. / Hallo, Claudia. / Wie geht's dir? / Danke, gut.

4 Hallo, Rob. – Hallo, Claudia.
Wie geht es Ihnen? – Danke, gut. Und Ihnen?
Guten Tag, ich bin Chris Bruckner. – Guten Tag, Frau Bruckner. Herzlich willkommen.
Wie geht's dir? – Gut, danke.
Sind Sie Herr Heinrich? – Ja, das bin ich.

5 **Sie:** Sie, Guten Tag, Frau; **du:** Hallo, Hallo

6 **Sie:** Sind, bin, ist
du: Bist, bin, bin, bin

7 1. Guten Tag, 2. Danke, gut, 3. Hallo, 4. Ich bin Felix.

8 1a, 2c, 3a

9 Das sind Sie. Das sind wir. Das seid ihr. Das ist sie (*Sing.*). Das bin ich. Das ist er. Das sind sie (*Pl.*).

10 Ich bin, Sind Sie, Bist du, Herr Heinrich ist, Wir sind, Seid ihr, Sind Sie

11 Grüß Gott. – Grüß Gott.; Hallo, ..., wie geht's? – Gut, und dir?; Grüezi. – Grüezi, Nina.

Workbook page 9 / Textbook page 8:
Guten Tag, Servus, Grüezi

1 (Norddeutschland:) Guten Tag. Hallo. Auf Wiedersehen. Tschüs.

2 (Bayern:) Grüß Gott. Griaß di. Auf Wiederschaun. Pfiat di.

3 (Österreich:) Grüß Gott. Servus. Baba.

4 (Schweiz:) Grüezi. Uf Widerluege. Salut.

Test

1. 1. Hello, Good morning, Good afternoon, 2. Good morning, 3. Hello, Hi, 4. How are you?, 5. Fine, thanks. 6. Goodbye.

2. 1. Nacht, 2. Wiedersehen, 3. Guten, 4. Guten, 5. Guten, 6. Tschüs

3. 1. bin, 2. bist, 3. ist, 4. ist, 5. ist, 6. Sind, 7. Sind, 8. Sind

4. 1. bin, 2. Bist, 3. Sind, 4. bin, 5. ist, 6. ist

Lesson 2

2 <u>Sind</u> Sie aus Ber<u>lin</u>, Herr <u>Hein</u>rich?

Ja, <u>klar</u>. Und <u>Sie</u>, <u>wo</u>her kommen <u>Sie</u>?

Aus <u>Ö</u>sterreich, ich bin aus <u>Wien</u>. Aber ich <u>lebe</u> in <u>Mün</u>chen. Schon <u>lange</u>.

Sind Sie <u>gern</u> in München?

Ja, <u>sehr</u> gern. Ich wohne schon <u>fünf</u> <u>Ja</u>hre dort.

Kennen Sie Ber<u>lin</u>?

<u>Ja</u>, aber nicht <u>gut</u>.

3 1. Sind, 2. kommen, 3. bin, 4. lebe, 5. Sind, 6. wohne

4 aus Berlin, in Berlin, aus Österreich, in München, fünf Jahre dort, Berlin nicht gut

5 1. Nein, ich bin aus Wien. 2. Ja, schon lange. 3. Ja, aber nicht gut.

6 1. Nein, aus München. 2. Ja, klar. 3. Ja, das bin ich.

8 lebt, wohnt, wohnen, kommt, kommen, kennt, Kennen

Lebt Pierre in Paris? – Ja, er lebt in Paris. / Er ist aus Paris.

Kennen Sie Paris? – Ja, aber nicht gut. / Ich kenne London gut.

9 sein, wohnen, heißen, kennen

10 kennst, kennt, leben, wohnst, wohnt, wohnen, heiße, heißen

11 Ich heiße ... (your name), Wie heißt ..., Er heißt ..., Wie heißen ..., Wir heißen ...,
Wie heißt ..., Karla und Fritz heißen ...

12 kommt Andrea – Sie kommt; Lebt Pierre – Pierre lebt; kommen Graziella und Paolo
– sie kommen; Wohnt Juan – Juan wohnt; Kennen Sie – ich kenne; Wohnt Elsbeta –
sie wohnt

Workbook page 15 / Textbook page 12:
Städte-Quiz

Hamburg, Köln, Leipzig, Augsburg, Bern, Zürich, Salzburg, Graz

D ist Deutschland. A ist Österreich. CH ist die Schweiz.

Test

1. 1. How are you? 2. Yes, of course. 3. Yes, I am.

2. 1. kommen, 2. leben / wohnen, 3. heißen, 4. sein, 5. kennen

3. 1. aus, 2. Kommen, 3. wohne, 4. Sie, 5. Kennen, 6. Kommen

4. 1. Woher kommen Sie? 2. Sind Sie aus Hamburg? 3. Wohnen Sie in München?
4. Kennen Sie Berlin? 5. Sind Sie Herr Müller? 6. Wie geht es Ihnen?

Lesson 3

1 a. Groß, b. Julian, c. Stuttgart, d. Berlin, e. 10543, f. Neue Straße 10, g. Deutschland, h. *Julian Groß*

der Name – name, der Vorname – first name, der Geburtsort – place of birth, die Adresse – address, der Ort – place, die Postleitzahl – postcode / zipcode, die Straße – street / road, das Land – country, die Unterschrift – signature

4 a1, b1, c2, d8 oder 3, e8 oder 3, f4, g5, h7, i6

5 der Ort, der Name, die Postleitzahl, der Vorname, die Straße, die Adresse, das Land

6 Adresse

8 der Pass – das Visum, der Name – der Vorname, der Ort – die Postleitzahl, männlich – weiblich, ledig – verheiratet, das Hotel – die Adresse, der Geburtsort – das Geburtsjahr, Datum – Unterschrift

10 in, in, aus, in

11 Argentinien, Australien, Belgien, Brasilien, Bulgarien, Großbritannien, Indien, Indonesien, Italien, Kroatien, Moldawien, Rumänien, Slowenien

12 Aus Russland, Aus Frankreich, Aus den USA, Aus Deutschland, Aus der Schweiz, Aus Japan

13 null, eins, zwei, drei, vier, fünf, sechs, sieben, acht, neun, zehn

14 70190, 80805, 76137, 60313, 69118, 20143

18 fünf, zwei, vier, neun

Workbook page 21 / Textbook page 16:
Ausländer in Deutschland

Entschuldigen Sie, woher sind Sie?
Aus Deutschland.
Aus Deutschland?
Ja, klar. Ich bin aus Berlin. Ich wohne hier.
Und wie heißen Sie?
Özcan Saglem.
Aha.

Test

1. 1. What's your name? 2. Where were you born? 3. Please spell it. 4. I'm divorced. 5. Where ... from? 6. Your passport number, please.

2. 1. das, 2. die, 3. die, 4. der, 5. der, 6. das

3. 1. verheiratet, 2. wohnen Sie, 3. Ihre Adresse, 4. kommen Sie, 5. die Pass-Nummer, 6. aus Österreich

4. 1. Müller, 2. Janssen, 3. Hamburg

Lesson 4

1 Wie geht's? – 1, 2, 4
Wie ist das Wetter? – 2, 3
Wie ist das Hotel? – 1, 2, 3
Wie war die Reise? – 1, 2, 4

2 Das <u>Wet</u>ter ist <u>auch</u> prima.
<u>Ja</u>, es ist <u>schön</u> und <u>sehr</u> <u>warm</u>. Wie ist es denn in <u>Mün</u>chen?
<u>Leider</u> <u>schlecht</u>. Es <u>regnet</u> schon <u>zwei</u> Tage.
Da haben Sie <u>hier</u> <u>Glück</u>. <u>Kenn</u>en Sie die Stadt?
<u>Nicht</u> sehr gut.
Dann machen wir eine <u>Stadt</u>rundfahrt. Vielleicht <u>morgen</u>?
<u>Ja</u>, <u>gerne</u>.

3 **Bruckner:** b, e, f, h; **Kühne:** a, c, d, g, i, j

4 a. gut, b. direkt im Zentrum, c. praktisch, d. nicht schlecht, e. in München,
f. nicht sehr gut.

6 **Richtig:** Frau A. wohnt im Hotel Amsterdam. – Frau A. wohnt im Amsterdam.
– Das Hotel ist sehr praktisch.

8 gut, gut, weit, praktisch, prima, schön, warm, schlecht, gut

9 Tag, Frau, Reise, Herr, Hotel, Zentrum, Wetter, München, Glück, Stadt,
Stadtrundfahrt

10 die Reise, das Zentrum, die Adresse, das Land, der Name, der Tag, die Stadt,
das Hotel, das Wetter, die Stadtrundfahrt, das Glück

11 Geschäft – es, Tag – er, Stadt – sie, Euro – er, Reise – sie, Haus – es, Auto – es,
Zeit – sie, Adresse – sie

12 gut, herzlich, prima, schön, warm, schlecht, geschieden, ledig, neu, richtig, langsam,
männlich, schnell, weiblich, falsch, kalt, negativ, praktisch, weit

13 Nein, das Wetter ist nicht schön. Nein, es regnet nicht. Nein, das Zentrum ist nicht
weit. Nein, das Hotel ist nicht praktisch. Nein, die Reise ist nicht prima.

17 der Name, das Land, der Familienstand, die Adresse, das Geburtsland, die Nationalität

Workbook page 27 / Textbook page 20:
Ländernamen

Neuseeland, England, Türkei, Russland, Deutschland, Österreich, China, Korea, Italien,
Brasilien
4 Korea, 9 Österreich, 7 China, 5 Deutschland, 8 Brasilien, 6 England, 10 Russland,
1 Neuseeland, 3 Türkei, 2 Italien, 11 Frankreich

Test

1. 1. How are you? 2. Very well. 3. Bad, I'm afraid.

2. 3 Es ist sehr warm. 1 Es ist windig. 5 Es ist kalt. 4 Die Sonne scheint. 6 Es regnet.
2 Es schneit.

3. 1. der, 2. die, 3. das, 4. die, 5. das, 6. das

4. 1., 3., 4., 5., 8.

5. 1. Nein, das ist nicht weit. 2. Nein, das ist nicht schön. 3. Nein, es ist nicht kalt.
4. Nein, es ist nicht windig. 5. Nein, es regnet nicht. 6. Nein, es schneit nicht.

Lesson 5

1 a2, b5, c1, d4, e3

3 Was, Wo, Wie lange, Wie, Wann

4 Die Fahrkarte kostet zwei Euro. – Robert und Claudia sind in Berlin. – Rosenheim ist
eine Kleinstadt. – Berlin ist eine Großstadt. – Niki arbeitet furchtbar viel / sehr viel.
– Robert arbeitet furchtbar wenig / sehr wenig / nicht viel.

5 heiße, ist, sind, ist, heißt

6 Zwei Euro. – Eine Stunde. – Super. – Mit der S-Bahn. – Spät. – Nein, furchtbar
wenig.

7 Eine Stunde, die Fahrkarte, eine Frage, ein Hotel, eine Großstadt, ein Bundesland

8 du: hast, arbeitest, fährst; er/sie/es: hat; arbeitet; fährt; ihr: arbeitet

9 die Minute, die Fahrkarte, die Großstadt, der Euro, die Kleinstadt, die Stunde,
die S-Bahn, das Auto

10 1 Fahrkarten, 2 Minuten, 3 Stunden, 4 Namen, 5 Länder, 6 Wörter

11 eine – Minuten, eine – Stunden, eine – Städte, eine – Großstädte, eine – Kleinstädte,
ein – Geschäfte, eine – S-Bahnen, ein – Autos

13 Stadt – Städte, Land – Länder, Wort – Wörter, Satz – Sätze, Pass – Pässe

14 in Bremen, schon ein Jahr dort, kennt

Workbook page 33 / Textbook page 24:
Nachbarländer

Dänemark, Polen, Tschechien, Österreich, die Schweiz, Frankreich, Luxemburg, Belgien,
die Niederlande

Test

1. 1. Thank you. 2. How much is it? 3. home, 4. little time, 5. terribly hard, 6. Sorry?

2. 1. die Stadt, 2. eine Minute, 3. eine Stunde, 4. die Fahrkarte, 5. das Wort, 6. ein Land

3. 1. Arbeitest, 2. Hast, 3. arbeiten, 4. Fahrt, 5. fahren, 6. kostet

4. 1. die, 2. die, 3. die, 4. der, 5. die, 6. das

5. 1. Stadt, 2. Wörter, 3. Sätze, 4. Land, 5. Pass, 6. Pässe

Lesson 6

1 a4, b5, c3, d1, e2, f7, g6

3 Berlin: wohnen, Rosenheim: wohnt, München: studiert

4 Wer, geboren, Jahre, Beruf, bei, Hobbys; Wer, aus, München, Student, Zeit, findet

5 Sie ist in Berlin geboren. – Sie ist 23 Jahre alt. – Sie ist Medien-Designerin von Beruf. – Sie arbeitet bei Art & Design. – Ihre Hobbys sind Reisen und Sprachen. – Robert kommt aus Rosenheim.

6 a2, b1, c5, d6, e3, f4

8 *Example:* Ich finde Claudia sympathisch.

9 1c, 2e, 3f, 4g, 5d, 6a, 7b

10 (ein)hundertfünfzig, fünfundzwanzig, dreiundsiebzig, fünfzehn, fünf, neunundneunzig

11 1. 089 – 46 37 49, 2. 040 – 77 88 90, 3. 030 – 307 26 50, 4. 069 – 32 56 80

Workbook page 39 / Textbook page 28:
Ein Schloss in Bayern

1. Im Süden von München, 2. 150 Kilometer, 3. 8 Euro

Test

1. 1. Kleinstadt, 2. vielen Dank, 3. Telefonnummer, 4. nach Hause, 5. Hobby, 6. interessant

2. 1. Er studiert. 2. Sie studiert in Hamburg. 3. Er ist in Deutschland geboren. 4. Er ist drei Jahre alt. 5. Wo arbeiten Sie? 6. Was sind Sie von Beruf?

3. 1. arbeitest, 2. studiert, 3. fahre, 4. kommst, 5. hast

4. 1. Wo, 2. Was, 3. Wo, 4. Wie, 5. Wie lange, 6. Was

5. 1. ist nicht in Deutschland geboren, 2. arbeitet, 3. schon fünf Jahre da

Lesson 7

1 Kaffee / Tee, Milch und Zucker, Milch / Zucker.

3 2, 4, 3, 1

4 1b, 2d, 3a, 4g, 5c, 6e, 7f

5 Leid, Mittag, gern, Kantine, Tee; DANKE

6 a. Ja, gerne. b. Tee, bitte. c. Ja, danke. d. Ja, bitte. e. Nur Milch, bitte. f. Ja, gerne.

7 a. Fahrkarte, b. Hobby, c. Sprache, d. Buchstabe, e. sympathisch, f. Informatik

8 liegt, gut, fünf Jahre, Herr, Chef, alt, Beruf

9 eine Kleinstadt, eine Handy-Nummer, ein Vorname, ein Land, eine Postleitzahl, ein Wort

10 ich: möchte, kann; du: nimmst, möchtest, kannst; er / sie: nimmt, kann; ihr: möchtet; sie / Sie: können

11 Möchten Sie, Kann ich, Kann ich, Möchten Sie, Kann ich, Möchten Sie, Können Sie, Können Sie

12 wo das Hotel, wann der Bus, wie der Herr, was die Fahrkarte, woher Herr Bünzli, wer Herr Heinrich

14 **kurz:** hat, dann, Stadt, schlecht, kommt, sind, Stunde; **lang:** haben, da, Jahr, Tee, schon, Sie, nur

15 Who is that please? ... – Wer ist dort bitte? ... / Is that Meier? ... – Ist dort Meier? ... / Is that Meier? ... Goodbye. – Ist dort Meier? ... Auf Wiederhören.

Workbook page 45 / Textbook page 32:
Kaffee trinken

In Deutschland, In Österreich, In der Schweiz

Test

1. 1. Tee, 2. Zitrone, 3. nichts, 4. Frau, 5. Beruf, 6. Süden
2. 1. That's OK. 2. Can I please ...? 3. I'd like ..., 4. OK? 5. I'm sorry. 6. Yes, of course.
3. 1. Möchten Sie, 2. Ich möchte, 3. Ich nehme, 4. Wir arbeiten, 5. Wer geht,
   6. Machen Sie, 7. Können wir, 8. kann
4. 1. eine, 2. ein, 3. eine, 4. eine, 5. eine, 6. ein, 7. eine, 8. ein

Lesson 8

1 arbeiten, kochen, trinken, essen, sprechen, fahren
3 zu Hause, prima, Spaß, Pause, recht, Hunger, Überraschung, Salat
4 Hunger und Durst
5 a. zu Hause, b. früher gegangen, c. viel, d. recht, e. Hunger, f. Spaghetti und Salat
6 Er ist, Er ist, Er hat, Die Arbeit hat, Er hat, Wir haben, Wir haben
7 a. Klasse! *oder* Prima! b. Na klar. c. Na klar. d. Na ja. *oder* Bestens. e. Na ja.
   f. Ach was. *oder* Na klar. g. Schade. *oder* Macht nichts.
8 Hause, gegangen, arbeitet, recht, und, gemacht, fahren, fährt
9 **G** = Fahrt ihr in die Stadt? Was heißt das? Hast du Hunger? Du hast recht. Wohin fährt die Bahn?
   V = Was hast du heute gemacht? Wo bist du geboren? Ich habe schon gegessen. Hast du gearbeitet? Ich bin früh nach Hause gegangen.
10 *lesen* – du liest, er/sie liest
   essen – du isst, er/sie isst
   haben – du hast, er/sie hat
   geben – du gibst, er/sie gibt
   fahren – du fährst, er/sie fährt
   nehmen – du nimmst, er/sie nimmt
   sprechen – du sprichst, er/sie spricht
11 Ich habe heute etwas gekocht. Da ist niemand. Nein, ich arbeite zu viel. Ich bin extra früher gegangen.

15 Hallo.
Wer ist dort bitte?
Hier Meyer.
Ist dort Meyer, Telefon 46 88 11?
Nein, hier Meyer, Telefon 46 77 11.
Oh, Entschuldigung.
Bitte sehr.

Workbook page 51 / Textbook page 36:
Sprichwörter

Kommt Zeit, kommt Rat. Der Apfel fällt nicht weit vom Stamm. Probieren geht über Studieren. Der Ton macht die Musik. Wer Sorgen hat, hat auch Likör.

Test

1. 1. recht, 2. dran, 3. Hunger, 4. Spaß, 5. nichts, 6. was
2. 1. Er ist extra früher gegangen. 2. Er arbeitet viel. 3. Sie hat recht. 4. Das ist eine Überraschung. 5. Wer hat gekocht? 6. Er hat Spaghetti gekocht.
3. 1. hast, 2. Ist, 3. Seid, 4. haben, 5. hat, 6. hast
4. 1. fährt, 2. isst, 3. nimmt, 4. gibt, 5. ist, 6. spricht

Lesson 9

1

das Wohnzimmer	der Balkon
	die Küche
der Flur	
	die Toilette
das Schlafzimmer	das Bad

3 1. im Zentrum, 2. zwei Zimmer mit Bad, 3. Dachwohnung, 4. im Wohnzimmer, 5. 550 Euro warm, 6. im Norden
4 haben wir, Ich habe, haben wir, Ich habe
5 a2, b4, c1, d3, e6, f5
6 1. 12 (zwölf), 2. 5 (fünf), 3. 45 (fünfundvierzig), 4. 10 (zehn) Euro; 1.050 ((ein)tausend(und)fünfzig) Euro
7 baden, kochen, schlafen, wohnen, arbeiten, fahren
8 Ich finde die Wohnung super. Ich finde das Bad praktisch. Ich finde den Balkon schön. Ich finde den Kaffee gut. Ich finde das Hotel schlecht.
9 Das praktische Bad. Der nette Markus. Das schlechte Hotel. Die sympathische Daniela. Die richtige Lösung.
10 1b, 2a, 3d, 4c, 5e, 6f
11 1. eine Kantine, 2. ein Bad, 3. ein Wohnzimmer, 4. ein Balkon, 5. eine Küche, 6. ein Schlafzimmer

12 Die Kantine, Das Bad, Das Wohnzimmer, Der Balkon, Die Küche, Das Schlafzimmer

13 die Kantine, das Bad, das Wohnzimmer, den Balkon, die Küche, das Schlafzimmer

14 eine Wohnung, eine Anzeige, eine Lösung, einen Salat, ein Büro

17 5 Euro, 99 Euro, 550 Euro, 2.500 Euro, 450 Euro, 250 Euro

Workbook page 57 / Textbook page 40:
Rätsel

A	= eins	K	= elf	U	= einundzwanzig
B	= zwei	L	= zwölf	V	= zweiundzwanzig
C	= drei	M	= dreizehn	W	= dreiundzwanzig
D	= vier	N	= vierzehn	X	= vierundzwanzig
E	= fünf	O	= fünfzehn	Y	= fünfundzwanzig
F	= sechs	P	= sechzehn	Z	= sechsundzwanzig
G	= sieben	Q	= siebzehn	Ä	= siebenundzwanzig
H	= acht	R	= achtzehn	Ö	= achtundzwanzig
I	= neun	S	= neunzehn	Ü	= neunundzwanzig
J	= zehn	T	= zwanzig	ß	= dreißig

Answer: Viel Glück!

Test

1. 1. flat, 2. advert, 3. garage, 4. 500 euros ... basic rent, 5. available immediately, 6. The flat is cosy.

2. 1. ein, ein, 2. einen, eine, ein, 3. keine, 4. einen, 5. Das, 6. Die

3. 1. gefunden, 2. gesagt, 3. gespart, gewohnt, 4. gelesen, 5. gemietet

4. 2 Zimmer, 35 qm, 600 Euro kalt, 0911 - 62424

Lesson 10

1 a2, b6, c5, d3, e1, f4

3 Frau Bruckner: a, c, d, f, Taxifahrer: b, e

4 Straße, Verkehr, Termin, Minuten, Wasser, Viertelstunde, Stau, Nummer, Euro, Quittung

5 a3, b4, c2, d1

8 **Singular:** 2. (Frage), 4.(Auto), 7. (Quittung), 8. (Anzeige)
Plural: 1. (Kinder), 3. (Städte), 5. (Uhren), 6. (Nummern)

9 das Hobby, die Adressen, das Kind, die Hotels, der Name, die Tage, die Autos, die Nummern, die Stunde, das Land, die Fragen

10 Es ist halb zwölf. Es ist Viertel nach vier. Es ist Viertel vor elf. Es ist ein Uhr. (= Es ist eins.) Es ist zehn nach neun. Es ist zwanzig vor zehn.

12 **lang:** viel, abends, Problem, Kanal; **kurz:** links, fast, schrecklich, morgens

Workbook page 63 / Textbook page 44:
Wie weit ist das von Frankfurt?

1 Oslo 1.099 km, 2 Stockholm 1.188 km, 3 Moskau 2.023 km, 4 Warschau 892 km,
5 Brüssel 316 km, 6 Bern 363 km, 7 Wien 598 km, 8 Lissabon 1.892 km,
9 Madrid 1.447 km, 10 Athen 1.803 km
Nach Moskau ist es weiter als nach Madrid. Nach Madrid ist es weiter als nach Oslo.
Nach Athen ist es weiter als nach Bern.

Test

1. 1. sind, 2. möchten, 3. Nach, 4. lange, 5. Stunde, 6. Quittung.
2. 1. The clock is wrong. 2. The clock is fast. 3. The clock is slow. 4. About 20 minutes.
5. Quarter past three. 6. Quarter to seven.
3. 1. fünfzehn Uhr zehn, 2. sechzehn Uhr fünfundfünfzig, 3. achtzehn Uhr fünfzehn,
4. neunzehn Uhr fünfundvierzig, 5. neun Uhr siebenunddreißig, 6. elf Uhr fünfundfünfzig
4. 1. die Städte, 2. die Taxis, 3. die Quittungen, 4. die Termine, 5. die Büros, 6. die
Anzeigen, 7. die Häuser, 8. die Nummern

Lesson 11

1 *Examples:* Fahren Sie gern mit dem Zug? – Ja, sehr gern. Zug fahren ist sehr gemütlich. / Fliegen Sie gern? – Nein, nicht so gern. Fliegen ist teuer. / Fahren Sie gern mit
dem Bus? Nein, nicht gern. Bus fahren dauert sehr lange.
3 11 Uhr, um 12 Uhr, um 12, heute Abend, sieben Uhr, halb acht, um halb acht,
Morgen
4 1. Herr Heinrich, Frau Bruckner und Herr Kühne, 2. Herr Kühne, 3. Wir möchten Sie
zum Essen einladen. 4. Um halb acht. 5. Sie fährt mit dem Zug. 6. Sechseinhalb
Stunden.
5 Nein, ich habe ... keine Firma. / keinen Aufzug. / keinen Keller. / kein Archiv. /
kein Sekretariat.
6 *nehmen:* den Vertrieb, *möchten:* einen Tag, *haben:* einen Bahnhof, *kennen:* die
Stunde, *mieten:* eine Straße
8 Uhr, mit, wenig, Mittags, Essen, halb
9 den Bus – der, die Bahn – die, den Zug – der, das Flugzeug – das, das Auto – das
10 eine Kantine – die, einen Aufzug – der, eine Pause – die, ein Hotel – das, eine
Dachwohnung – die
11 einen Termin, den Bus und die Bahn, einen Kaffee, den Hafen, den Reichstag, einen
Ausflug
12 kein Tee, keine Pension – ein Hotel, keine Telefonnummer – ein Passwort, kein
Vorname – ein Nachname, kein Land – ein Erdteil, keine Vorwahlnummer – eine
Postleitzahl

13 kein Auto, fliege nicht, nicht gern, nicht mit dem Auto, keine Zeit, komme nicht, keine Frage

15 **1. Silbe (1ˢᵗ syllable):** Straße, Quittung, Nummer, morgens, Reise, machen, Handy, Zimmer, Mittag, München, Norden, gestern, Frage, Vorschlag
2. Silbe (2ⁿᵈ syllable): Verkehr, Termin, Beruf, Geschäft, Besuch, Berlin

16 **1. Silbe (1ˢᵗ syllable):** Stadtrundfahrt, Anzeige, Telefon, arbeiten, Fahrkarte
2. Silbe (2ⁿᵈ syllable): Adresse, sympathisch, Kantine, Geburtsort, Grammatik
3. Silbe (3ʳᵈ syllable): –

17 **1. Silbe (1ˢᵗ syllable):** –
2. Silbe (2ⁿᵈ syllable): besichtigen, Entschuldigung
3. Silbe (3ʳᵈ syllable): buchstabieren, Informatik;
4. Silbe: interessant, Information, geradeaus

Workbook page 69 / Textbook page 48:
Buchstaben-Labyrinth

Wann haben Sie Zeit? Ich moechte (= möchte) Sie zum Essen einladen.

Test

1. 1. invitation, 2. by train, 3. It's fun. 4. invite someone to dinner, 5. this evening, 6. suggestion

2. 1. haben, 2. einladen, 3. nehmen, 4. fahren, 5. gehen, 6. haben/machen

3. 1. ein – kein, 2. einen – keinen, 3. eine – keine, 4. einen – keinen, 5. eine – keine, 6. einen – keinen

4. 1. den Hafen, 2. den Bus, 3. den Stau, 4. den Zug, 5. den Aufzug, 6. die Kantine, 7. den Raum, 8. die Arbeit

Lesson 12

1 2 der Empfang, 7 die IT-Abteilung, 1 die Buchhaltung, 8 die Redaktion, 5 das Lager, 3 das Informationszentrum, 4 die Kantine, 6 der Konferenzraum
Words that come from English: Controlling, IT, Produktion, Marketing

3 A (Informationszentrum), E (Empfang und Redaktionen), D (Buchhaltung), F (IT-Abteilung), B (Controlling), C (Kantine)

5 Wir haben, Dann haben wir, Wir sind, Dann habe ich, Das Lager habe ich, Um 12 sind

6 1f, 2c, 3e, 4a, 5b, 6d

8 4 Montag, 5 Dienstag, 6 Mittwoch, 7 Donnerstag, 8 Freitag, 9 Samstag / Sonnabend, 10 Sonntag

9 Wir arbeiten bis elf Uhr. Dann machen wir eine Pause. Um 11 Uhr 15 machen wir eine Firmenbesichtigung. Die Firmenbesichtigung dauert bis 12. Um 12 gehen wir in die Kantine. Wir essen bis eins. Dann arbeiten wir bis 3. Um 3 machen wir eine Stadtrundfahrt. Um 7 sind wir im Hotel zurück.

10 Jetzt machen wir eine Firmenbesichtigung. Um 12 Uhr komme ich in die Kantine. Heute Abend habe ich Zeit. Morgen fahre ich zurück nach München. Vielleicht nehme ich den Zug. Dann rufe ich an.

13 **1. Silbe** (1ˢᵗ **syllable**): Erdgeschoss, Firmenbesichtigung
2. Silbe (2ⁿᵈ **syllable**): Empfang
3. Silbe (3ʳᵈ **syllable**): Redaktion, gegenüber, Konferenzräume
4. Silbe (4ᵗʰ **syllable**): geradeaus, Informationszentrum

Workbook page 75 / Textbook page 52:
Kleine Tipps

Richtig: 1. Man schüttelt sich die Hand bei Geburtstagen und Festen. Geschäftspartner schütteln sich die Hand.
2. *Mahlzeit* sagt man nur mittags bei der Arbeit. Der Gruß ist hässlich, sagen viele.
3. Pünktlichkeit ist in Deutschland wichtig. Man sagt: *Tut mir Leid, dass ich zu spät komme. / Ich komme leider ein paar Minuten zu spät.*

Test

1. 1. Konferenzraum, 2. Kantine, 3. Einladung, 4. Lager, 5. Informationszentrum, 6. Redaktion
2. 1. Hier ist kein Platz. 2. Ich glaube nicht. 3. Da geradeaus. 4. Das macht Spaß. 5. Ich verstehe.
3. 1. Heute besichtigen wir den Hafen. 2. Um eins nehmen wir den Bus. 3. Morgen haben wir Raum 3. 4. Bis 18 Uhr ist das Casino geöffnet. 5. Am Vormittag besichtigen wir die Firma. 6. Mittwoch fahre ich wieder zurück.
4. mögen, du magst, er/sie mag / geben, du gibst, er/sie gibt / fahren, du fährst, er/sie fährt / nehmen, du nimmst, er/sie nimmt / schlafen, du schläfst, er/sie schläft
5. 1. Berlin, 2. Circa 30 Euro, 3. Zentrum, 4. S-Bahn, 5. Ja

Lesson 13

3. Brot oder ein Brötchen, Müsli, nur Brot und Butter, einen Löffel, noch einen Teller, mein Messer und meine Gabel, ein Ei, Eier esse ich nicht
4. geschlafen, spät, weg, gleich, Brot, Magst
5. Möchtest, möchtest, mag, mag, mag, möchte
6. mein Bruder, deine Schwester, Meine Schwester, deine Geschwister, deine Eltern, Meine Eltern
8. früh, Frühstück, Mittag, Eltern, Geschwister
9. Test, Ei, Dachwohnung, Eltern, Wort, Sprache
10. kein Auto, keine Uhr, keine Geschwister, keine Zeit, keine Semesterferien, keinen Hunger

11. deine Fahrkarte, dein Handy, dein Kaffee, dein Frühstück, mein Bruder – meinen Bruder, meine Schwester – meine Schwester
12. nicht dein Frühstück – mein Frühstück, nicht deine Schwester – meine Schwester, nicht deine Fahrkarte – meine Fahrkarte, nicht dein Auto – mein Auto, nicht deine Uhr – meine Uhr, nicht dein/mein Problem – mein/dein Problem
13. Niki heißt Bat mit Familiennamen. Er wohnt und arbeitet in Berlin und ist auch hier geboren. Deshalb ist nur der Familienname Chinesisch, nicht der Vorname. Er spricht auch kein Chinesisch. Aber er möchte die Sprache gern lernen. Die Eltern sind 1960 nach Deutschland gekommen. Jetzt haben sie ein chinesisches Restaurant. Das ist das Restaurant in der Hafenstraße. Das Essen dort ist sehr gut, sagt man.

Workbook page 81 / Textbook page 56:
Wörtersalat

Länder und Kontinente: Australien, Spanien, Korea, Polen, Italien, Japan, Europa, Asien, Deutschland
Familie: Tante, Onkel, Sohn, Mädchen, Junge, verheiratet, Großeltern, Eltern, Vater, Mutter, Tochter, Opa, Oma
Jahr, Jahreszeit, Woche und Tag: Frühling, Freitag, Sonnabend, Donnerstag, Sommer, Sonntag, Montag, Wochenende, Mittwoch, Dienstag
Essen und Trinken: Restaurant, Tasse, Milch, Tee, Käse, Kaffee, Marmelade
Berufe: Regisseur, Hausfrau, Hausmann, Maurer, Maler, Arzt
Wohnung: Aufzug, Bad, Wohnzimmer, Balkon, Zimmer, Flur
Stadt: Schule, Tourist, Taxifahrer, Zentrum, Zug, Bahnhof, Auto, Bahn, Flughafen, Hafen, Haltestelle

Test

1. 1. Christian has already left. 2. Tell me ... are you hungry? 3. Jan is still in school. 4. What do you think? 5. By the way ... 6. Really?
2. 1. Vater, 2. Schwester, 3. Opa, 4. Sohn, 5. Tante, 6. Schwiegermutter, 7. Frau
3. 1. dein, 2. dein, 3. dein, 4. dein, 5. deine, 6. deine
4. 1. Möchtest, 2. mag, 3. mag, 4. Möchtest, 5. Magst, 6. mag

Lesson 14

1	Monika Freud (Oma) Helmut Freud (Opa) Thomas Bergmann (Vater) Beatrice Bergmann (Mutter) Ralf Bergmann (Bruder) Katrin Bergmann (Schwester) Claudia Bergmann

3 3, 2, 1, 4

4 Wir waren, Das war, Wir hatten, Niki und Claudia waren, Wie war, Hattet ihr

5 1. Katrin ist die Schwester von Claudia. Sie ist Regisseurin. 2. Robert findet eine Regisseurin interessant. 3. Robert spricht gut Englisch, aber nicht perfekt. 4. Robert, Claudia und Niki waren in England. Sie waren in einer Sprachenschule. Sie haben Englisch gelernt. 5. Claudias Mutter hat gekocht.

6 a1, b3, c2, d4, e5

8 Spargel mit Butter und Kartoffeln

9 waren, waren, hatte, war, waren, hatte, war

10 es, ihn, sie, sie, ihn, sie

11 Lieblingsstadt, Lieblingsbruder, Lieblingsschwester, Lieblingsfilm, Lieblingshotel, Lieblingsregisseur, Lieblingszimmer

12 Tschechien - Tschechisch, Polen - Polnisch, Russland - Russisch, Türkei - Türkisch, Japan - Japanisch, Spanien - Spanisch, Italien - Italienisch, China - Chinesisch, Korea - Koreanisch, Österreich - Österreichisch, Schweiz - Schweizerisch, Mexiko - Mexikanisch, Ungarn - Ungarisch, Griechenland - Griechisch

Workbook page 87 / Textbook page 60:
Das mögen wir!

a4, b3, c5, d1, e2, f6

Test

1. 1. Französisch, 2. Polnisch, 3. Österreichisch, 4. Türkisch, 5. Australisch, 6. Chinesisch, 7. Slowenisch, 8. Italienisch

2. 1. hatte, 2. hatte, 3. waren, 4. hatte, 5. war, 6. waren

3. 1. es, 2. sie, 3. es, 4. sie, 5. sie, 6. sie

Lesson 15

1 Robert – Student, Claudia – Medien-Designerin, Claudias Mutter – Malerin, Claudias Vater – Controller, Claudias Schwester – Regisseurin, Claudias Bruder – Schüler

3 1. Er war bei Claudias Eltern. 2. Er ist Ingenieur. 3. Sie ist Malerin. 4. Er geht noch zur Schule. 5. Sie heißt Katrin. 6. Er findet sie interessant.

4 Das ist Claudias Bruder. Das ist Claudias Schwester. Das ist Claudias Mutter. Das ist Claudias Großvater. Das ist Claudias Vater. Das ist Claudias Freund.

5 waren, sind, ist Ingenieur, ist Malerin, ist bald fertig, war auch da, ist Regisseurin

8 *Example:*
Liebe Eltern,
herzliche Grüße aus Rom. Ich bin noch im Hotel, aber ich habe bald eine Wohnung.
Sie ist sehr klein, aber das reicht.
Liebe Grüße
Martin

9 Ralfs Mutter, Maxis Eltern, Maries Bruder, Frau Lehmanns Tochter, Herrn Müllers
Sohn, Birgits Auto

10 c, d, e, a, b, g, f

11 Regisseur – Regisseurin, Maler – Malerin, Studentin – Studentin, Übersetzerin –
Übersetzerin, Ingenieur – Ingenieurin, Frisör – Frisörin, Medien-Designer – Medien-
Designerin, Schornsteinfeger – Schornsteinfegerin, Hausmann – Hausfrau,
Handwerker – Handwerkerin, Kellner – Kellnerin, Notarzt – Notärztin, Informatiker
– Informatikerin, Techniker – Technikerin, Lehrer – Lehrerin, Schüler – Schülerin,
Arzt – Ärztin, Taxifahrer – Taxifahrerin, Verkäufer – Verkäuferin, Koch – Köchin,
Rechtsanwalt – Rechtsanwältin, Kfz-Mechaniker – Kfz-Mechanikerin, Redakteur –
Redakteurin, Busfahrer – Busfahrerin

Workbook page 93 / Textbook page 64:
Berufe

Taxifahrer – Taxifahrerin, Lehrer – Lehrerin, Frisör – Frisörin, Verkäufer – Verkäuferin,
Student – Studentin, Politiker – Politikerin, Maurer – ./., Schornsteinfeger –
Schornsteinfegerin, Arzt – Ärztin, Hausfrau – Hausmann, Geschäftsmann – Geschäftsfrau

Test

1. 1. Franz ist Übersetzer. 2. Ulrike ist Ärztin. 3. Tommy ist Taxifahrer. 4. Steffi ist
Schülerin. 5. Frau Sommer ist Malerin. 6. Herr Gruber ist Verkäufer.

2. 1. die Politikerin, 2. der Geschäftsmann, 3. die Ärztin, 4. der Verkäufer,
5. die Studentin, 6. die Ingenieurin

3. 1. Stefans Vater, 2. Filips Schwester, 3. Frau Meiers Tochter, 4. Annas Tante,
5. Ulrikes Freundin, 6. Katharinas Familie

4. 1. die Studentinnen, 2. die Ärztinnen, 3. die Freundinnen, 4. die Pilotinnen,
5. die Übersetzerinnen, 6. die Politikerinnen

5. 1. sind im Hotel, 2. Abend, 3. um halb acht, 4. eine halbe Stunde, 5. um neun Uhr

Training von Wortschatz und Grammatik!

Ein Handgriff – eine Lösung: Mit den *Wheels* haben Sie schnell den richtigen Dreh raus – und das bei allen Fragen rund um Wortschatz, Grammatik und anderen wichtigen Themen. Ideal zum Mitnehmen und Lernen unterwegs!

Wheels
Durchmesser 19 cm, vierfarbig, aus stabilem Plastik

Adjektive
ISBN 978–3–19–949546–8

Akkusativ oder Dativ?
ISBN 978–3–19–909546–0

der, die, das
ISBN 978–3–19–939546–1

Flirt-Trainer
ISBN 978–3–19–989546–6

Deutsch ... in Österreich
ISBN 978–3–19–719546–9

Deutsch ... in der Schweiz
ISBN 978–3–19–789546–8

Modalverben
ISBN 978–3–19–959546–5

Präpositionen
ISBN 978–3–19–929546–4

Schimpfen und Fluchen
ISBN 978–3–19–999546–3

Unregelmäßige Verben
ISBN 978–3–19–919546–7

Die *Wheels Plus*-Pakete enthalten zusätzlich ein Booklet mit bis zu 22 abwechslungsreichen Übungen, die mit Hilfe des beigefügten *Wheels* gelöst werden können.

Wheels Plus
Booklet (12 Seiten) + Wheel

der, die, das
ISBN 978–3–19–769546–4

Unregelmäßige Verben
ISBN 978–3–19–969546–2

Die *Wortschatzbox Deutsch als Fremdsprache* vermittelt mit dem bewährten Karteikartensystem die 1.000 häufigsten Vokabeln der Niveaustufe A1. Auf der Vorderseite der Karteikarte steht das deutsche Wort und alles, was Sie hierzu wissen müssen sowie meist ein typisches Anwendungsbeispiel, in das Sie die Vokabel in der richtigen Form eintragen können. Auf der Rückseite können Sie überprüfen, ob Ihr Eintrag korrekt ist und die Bedeutung des Wortes in Ihrer Muttersprache hinzufügen. Zur Kontrolle dient Ihnen die alphabetische Wortliste im Begleitheft.

Wortschatzbox
Deutsch als Fremdsprache – A1

1 Kartenblock (500 Karten)
Je 1 Begleitheft Englisch, Französisch, Italienisch, Polnisch, Spanisch, und Türkisch (je 16 Seiten)
ISBN 978–3–19–007915–5

Die Wortschatzbox ist auch erhältlich für die Niveaustufen A2 und B1 – jeweils zusätzlich mit Begleitheft für russische Deutschlerner.

www.hueber.de/deutsch-lernen